CHRISTIAN MARRIAGE

IS VOLUME

54

OF THE

Twentieth Century Encyclopedia of Catholicism

UNDER SECTION

V

THE LIFE OF FAITH

IT IS ALSO THE

31ST

VOLUME IN ORDER OF PUBLICATION

Edited by **HENRI DANIEL-ROPS** *of the Académie Française*

CHRISTIAN MARRIAGE

By JEAN DE FABRÈGUES

Translated from the French by ROSEMARY HAUGHTON

HAWTHORN BOOKS · PUBLISHERS · *New York*

First Edition, December, 1959

NIHIL OBSTAT

Johannes M. T. Barton, D.D., L.S.S.

Censor Deputatus

IMPRIMATUR

E. Morrogh Bernard

Vicarius Generalis

Westmonasterii, die XVIII SEPTEMBRIS MCMLIX

CONTENTS

INTRODUCTION   9

I. THE PURPOSE OF MARRIAGE   13
    The Laws of Christian Marriage Are the
      Laws of Human Nature   13
    The True Human Instinct Is Not to Love the
      Lowest   17
    Don Juan, or Desire Without Remedy   19
    The Flesh Is Much More than the Flesh   23
    Married Union Is Necessary in Order to Be-
      come an Integrated Human Being   26
    The Married Couple Share in the Working
      Out of God's Plan   27
    Marriage Is a Sacrament Because It Is Also
      a Sacred Act   30
    The Ends of Christian Marriage and Human
      Dignity in Married Union   32
      The Two Ends of Marriage Are Linked   32
      Procreation the Primary End Emphasized
        by the Old Testament   34
      The End of "Mutual Help" Is Made Clear
        in the New Testament   36
      The Thomist Analysis Shows That the
        Sexual Act Is Good in Itself   37
      The Twofold Means of the Perfection of
        the Couple   39
      The End of the Partner's Perfection Is
        Secondary in Relation to the End of
        Creation Within God's Plan for the
        World   40
      Fulfilment and Perfection by Transcend-
        ence in Creation Through Love   42

II. THE LAWS OF CHRISTIAN MARRIAGE AND
MARRIED LIFE 45
The Laws of Christian Marriage Are Divine 45
The Partners Make Their Marriage by Their
Free Consent to These Laws 47
The Grace of the Sacrament 49
The Heart of Christian Marriage 52
The Church Alone Can Lawfully Define the
Laws of Marriage 57
The Church's Marriage Laws Not Recent 58
Indissolubility Also Serves Best the "Ful-
filment" of Personality 60
The Act of Love Must Involve the Accept-
ance of All Its Consequences 65
The Church Forbids Contraceptive Practices 67
Regulation of Births 68
Within the Limits of Respect for the Mar-
riage Union 68
An Intention Contrary to the Marriage
Vow 69
Subordinated to the Good of the Couple,
the Family and Society and to Respect
for Nature 70
Respect for Love Dictates the Church's
Attitude 72
The "Wrath of God" Defends Men from
Themselves 74

III. EROS AND AGAPE 78
Where Is Love? 78
Christian Love Gives Honour to the Flesh 80
The Flesh Expresses the Whole Being 83
Christ Delivered Love from Its Bondage 85
Marriage As the Image of Christ's Union
with the Church 86
The Whole Community 88
Sex Education 90
Education in General 91
The Dignity of Marriage As the Creator of
Souls 92

CONCLUSION   94
    The True Rights of the Child   94
    The Boy Who Killed to Find His Mother   96
    Maternal Affection Indespensable:
      UNESCO's Inquiry   97
    The Meaning of Adolescent Crime   99
    Respect for Human Nature Involves Respect
      for the Family   102
    The Family Is Our Point of Contact with
      the World   105
    The Family, Source of Joy   106
    Man's Fulfilment   107

SELECT BIBLIOGRAPHY   110

INTRODUCTION

Home of wildest hope and deepest despair, of the most unbridled selfishness and sometimes of the most absolute renunciation, of the dreariest and most bitter failure but also of life-giving fulfilment: marriage is all these things because it is the place where the greatest thing in heaven and earth breaks through into our lives, the hard baffling outcrop of what we call love. It is all these things at once because it is the point, mysterious and yet always inescapably there, at which flesh and spirit meet, struggle, perceive and recognize each other, so that they merge in a unity without end or stand opposed in a hatred without pity. It is the place where our condition is made clear, is lit up, where we suffer distress and return to peace; the point at which we take, or refuse to take, our place in the procession that never ends; the caravan whose journey has no stopping place, our place which, however humble, can belong to no one else in the simple yet mysterious business which is called life.

So there is really no morality of marriage: that would leave out too much. Rather is there a mystery of marriage which is the mystery of the meeting of Flesh and Spirit itself. And there is a theology of marriage.

Every time that love is born, which means every time that hope is reborn, at every embrace, God is mysteriously present. He is there, close even to those who have refused him. He is there in the ever unfulfilled quest of Don Juan, nearer perhaps than at any moment of our lives for this perpetual emptiness at which the collector of "conquests" hurls himself, was carved out by God, it is only the impress of his own image. He is there in the seed which is passed on or annihilated.

Christian marriage, then, is not marriage according to a morality, in the sense in which we might want to create a social morality, a morality of expediency, a useful morality. Christian marriage claims our allegiance to the laws of love itself, for they are the laws of life. But this life is not truly life unless it is God's life: if it is not transformed into the life of God it ceases to be a life at all.

Anyone who talks as if Christian law, as if even God himself and his demands, were something extra added on to life and its laws shows that he has not even begun to understand what the Christian faith has to say about the life of love. It is love itself which demands of man and woman what the Christian faith teaches them. It is the law of their love itself, not because God has framed the law but rather because he himself is the faith that binds them in love. It is useless to try to distinguish between God and love; they are one.

But the human soul cries in despair: it is impossible, I cannot, you want to separate me from love itself and even from God—the law is too hard. What prideful folly! The law is indeed "too hard" for the flesh. But the law itself is a law of love, it is Love in human love and, far better than the human lover, it knows with a detailed and accurate science that takes him unawares, what he is. It takes him just as he is and where he is, and bears him on to the place where he should be. All that is needed (but that is essential) is that he should not refuse it. The rejection of this law means the rejection of oneself; for it is the law of man's very being, the law of that flesh from which he thought it might separate him.

A great contemporary Catholic writer has written a wonderful book in which he tried to describe the suffering of a Christian: for him this suffering consists in the fact that God separates the Christian from the flesh. But the reverse is true: it is the flesh that separates us from God, if we prefer it to God. But look at the end of it all: if we accept the other law, which is the law of the flesh alone, it will possess us entirely. It is the law of the unbridled flesh that kills man. The Christian suffers really not because God separates him from the flesh but because the flesh separates him from the true life which is in God.

Once this is clear it is necessary first of all to defend Christian marriage against its caricatures. The best way to defend it will be to see exactly what it is. It will help if we notice three outstanding points.

Christian marriage is not necessarily doomed to boredom and mediocrity. On the contrary, a marriage that is dull and mediocre is not really—or at least not completely—a Christian marriage, since it has come adrift from real life.

Christian marriage is not easy: on the contrary it is particularly difficult to make a success of it, just as beauty and truth are hard to find. But along the difficult path is light and grace, so much so that, taking a long view, this hard road is the only passable one, the others lead to dead ends, or to the edge of the precipice.

Christian marriage is never a success, in the special sense in which no man is a hero to his valet, and no saint if he thinks himself one. The flesh is always the flesh, the absolute is always the absolute, the life of man is always divided and shared, suffering is still suffering, his discontent is born with him—and is a blessing because it is the sign of God's presence, it proclaims him and leads to him.

But along this boulder-strewn road whose end is not on earth, light and grace bring to those who walk on it such joy and firm hope as can never be found along the other roads that boast of being, or believe themselves to be, the ways of love; for this, precisely, is the way of being, the one which is conformed to what we are in our inmost selves, because it is the path traced out by God according to the original design of the being whose loving creator he is.

"It is not well that man should be without companionship," God said, "I will give him a mate of his own kind" (Gen. 2. 18). Not well for whom? Not well for man himself, not well *absolutely*. Neither among the birds of the air nor among the wild beasts that God created was a mate "of his own kind" to be found for man. Therefore, God created woman and man cried out: "Here at last is bone that comes from mine, flesh that comes from mine ... that is why a man is destined to leave father and mother, and cling to his wife instead, so that the two become one flesh" (Gen. 2. 23, 24). Such is the origin of marriage, in the place in which nature is born directly from the will of God: one woman for one man, one man for one woman.

So the play begins, a play which will only finish at the last day in the final reconciliation. For like every human action in the development towards the last end, like every free act, marriage is a drama, not yet finished but at each moment full of meaning that floods the stage with light.

Which of us has not met, whether on the street or in a book, one of those wonderful couples whose glance, one to the other and one on the other, holds the peace and joy of fulfilment? Sometimes, even often, it is exchanged between people who have not loved each other in the sense in which men usually use that word: they have not been to each other the adorable revelation, the clear answer, to undefined expectation. And when this is the case it sometimes matters little whether or not flesh has found a voice. Whether its song has been sung or whether, in the silence of the senses, other harmonies have been heard, is of no account. They have gazed together towards the same horizons, have been nourished by the same truths, built together, suffered together.

Fulfilment in marriage does not spring only from what we call love. Look further: there are many kinds of love, and married fulfilment springs from that life-giving communion which is much more than a common will, more than ideas in common. It is a gradual opening out to receive life, the very heart of life, so that in its deepest reality it may continue to reach out towards the future—towards eternity.

CHAPTER I

THE

PURPOSE OF MARRIAGE

THE LAWS OF CHRISTIAN MARRIAGE ARE THE LAWS OF HUMAN NATURE

Is this natural act really so great a thing? It is great—the very greatest after the acts of God himself, being in fact one of these acts—precisely because it is *natural*. It is nature itself, the progress of nature, the handing on of life itself. And God is the glorious creator of nature: it is, and though stained with sin it remains, a glorious creation, made to be saved and so already saved. Those who do not believe in the Christian God must never be allowed to think that Christians despise nature and that love which is its voice. The whole grandeur of God's design is shown in this natural act which he has made in some way a reflection, an imitation, of his own power, in which nature in its turn becomes the creator of Being. It is a staggering thought, and it is the reason why there is from the first no point in asking whether marriage belongs to nature or to God. It belongs to God because it belongs to nature; God, that is, does not exact our submission to a sort of arbitrary whim of his, to the demands of a rule foreign to our nature and to the good of that nature. The laws of life in marriage are born of the essence of marriage, they are simply the expression of what is necessary to marriage as the deepest union of two human beings.

But if marriage is a natural thing then conversely and much more deeply, it is a divine thing. This fitness in nature, if it is fitting, exists because God has willed it so, and therefore it is infinitely good, beyond anything that we can imagine, since this is the way by which God has willed to lead the greater part of the human race.

But is what we find in nature truly marriage? What we find in human nature—not just in animal nature—is truly marriage. From the birth of the incarnate Word we date our knowledge of what man is, of how great is his dignity and, as a result, how heavy are the demands it makes; among all the reasons we have for gratitude for the Christian faith, one of the greatest is this gift: the knowledge of what love is and what love demands.

"Union in marriage," wrote Leo XIII,[1] "is not the work nor the invention of man: it is God himself, the supreme author of nature, who has, from the beginning, provided with due order for the propagation of the human race and the constitution of the family by this union; it is he who, by the law of grace, wished to make it even greater by marking it with the divine seal of the sacrament."

Pius XI, repeating the very words of Leo XIII, continued in his encyclical *Casti Connubii*: "Such is the doctrine of Holy Scripture, such is the constant tradition of the universal Church, such is the solemn definition of the Council of Trent, which, borrowing the very words of Holy Scripture, teaches and confirms that the perpetual indissolubility of marriage, its unity and immutability, spring from God who is its author." It is in man's nature itself, just as it was willed and created by God, that the reason is to be found for what we call marriage—a unique and indissoluble union.

[1] From the letter *Ci Siamo*, June 1st, 1889, to the bishops of Piedmont, congratulating them on their protest against a new law forbidding the celebration of a religious marriage ceremony before the conclusion of civil formalities.

From the human act which is the pivotal act of marriage, the act of love itself, a child will be born if its consequences are not frustrated by the will and deed of man. That is its purpose, and we shall see later that to refuse this consequence is to strike at the very nature of man. What is a child? The human race reaching out towards the future. To refuse this forward movement is to stop life, to refuse life. But to accept it without surrounding this miniature man with the things he needs in order to become a true man—love so that he may be loving, teaching so that he may be rational, may be conscious in his turn of the flame that he bears, of the torch that he must hand on—to deprive him of these is to create a man while refusing him what is necessary if he is to reach manhood. If a child is to have love, education, reason, balance, a sense of mission and of his responsibility to the future, he must have the stable environment created by married unity of purpose. This need is at the root of married life, from its very beginning, a life of mysterious unity whose complexity we only discover little by little, in the measure in which we come to realize *what man is*. But it is there from the first, in the nature of things, that nature which is the voice and the will of God himself.

Leo XIII in his encyclical *Arcanum*, Pius XI in *Divini Redemptoris* and in *Casti Connubii*, Pius XII twenty times over—the popes have not ceased to repeat these things in the face of all "modern" doctrines, in the teeth of nineteenth-century "liberalism", of twentieth-century Marxism and eugenics. And they have made it clear that in doing so they were merely upholding the changeless doctrine of the Church, explaining the words of the book of Genesis, reiterating the definitions of the Council of Trent.

In 1942 Pius XII addressed a gathering of young married couples, and after reminding his hearers of Christ's words reported by St Matthew, that man should not put asunder what God has joined, he asked them: "Why then did God unite man and woman in Paradise?" And he gave the answer:

"It was not only so that they might care for that garden of happiness, but also, we assert with that great doctor Thomas Aquinas, that it was because they were destined through marriage to bring forth and educate children, and further, to establish the life of the family community."

This then, in God's plan expressed in nature, is the origin of marriage: the child and the family community. As early as 1741 Benedict XIV was insisting on this in the wake of the Council of Trent: "That the marriage bond, instituted by God, must be perpetual and indissoluble, because it is a natural duty, in the interests of the education of the children and for the safety of the other goods in marriage; and further because, as a sacrament of the Church, the boldness of man must not dare to dissolve it, for our Saviour himself declared it with his own lips when he said: 'What God has joined together let no man put asunder.'" When the popes recalled the foundation of the unique and indissoluble bond of marriage in nature and the will of God they were aware that they were only repeating the teaching of Christ himself. Leo XIII in the encyclical *Arcanum* quoted the words of Christ from St Matthew's Gospel: "And I tell you that he who puts away his wife, not for any unfaithfulness of hers, and so marries another, commits adultery; and he too commits adultery who marries her after she has been put away" (Matt. 19. 9). And Pius XI in the encyclical *Casti Connubii* refers to the text of St Paul's letter to the Ephesians (5. 32, 33) in which he says: "That is why a man will leave his father and mother and will cling to his wife, and the two will become one flesh. Yes, those words are a high mystery, and I am applying them here to Christ and his Church. Meanwhile, each of you is to love his wife as he would love himself, and the wife is to pay reverence to her husband."

We shall come back to this later on, for it concerns marriage as the symbol of the very union of Christ and his Church, and at this point it assures a vivid sense of the permanence of the marriage bond.

THE TRUE HUMAN INSTINCT IS NOT TO LOVE THE LOWEST

For a moment we can hear a rising murmur of protest: The *natural* thing is not marriage but *instinct*, the instinct that drives a man and woman into each other's arms, that demands union. How can we refuse the demands of that instinct? They are everywhere, in the being and the very scent of things, in our books and our traditions, in the eyes of boys and girls, in the joy of engaged couples and in the fierce flame of adulterous love.

What is instinct? "Instinct is not the name of a fact," writes Dr Rudolf Allers,[2] "but the brief summary of a theory. We can never observe instinct, but only actions or experiences, and ways of behaving which we relate to a particular common cause. Biology never observes instinct, it merely records modes of behaviour. Neither does introspection show us instinct, we have simply the experience of being impelled to perform certain actions." This learned medical psychologist shows that what we find in man is the complex phenomenon of *personality*, a combination of elements of which the instincts are part only, an "elemental" part precisely.

The doctrine that human nature is only truly itself when these instinctive elements are "liberated", given free rein, was popular at the end of the nineteenth century and the beginning of the twentieth. If this is true, then the true man is not only the child or the savage but equally the lunatic, the madman, the man who is the slave of his passions, the criminal. Such a conclusion is itself a judgement on the thesis: it is not instinct that makes a nature *human*. If it is human, in order to be human our nature must be the ordered combination of these instincts in a human personality. The true expression of man is not ungoverned instinct, but instinct ordered and

[2] Dr Allers, a professor at the University of Vienna, has, like Charles Baudouin in another context, thought out the whole of psychoanalysis from the Christian point of view. This extract is from a special number of *Etudes Carmélitaines* (April, 1936) on the subject of love.

guided by the whole personality. It would be true to say that the will to order one's instincts as a personality is the instinct proper to man. Human nature is not an unleashed eroticism but love which is conscious of the conditions of a truly human love. The distinctive thing about man in this field as in all others is not a love for the lowest but for the highest. The specifically human thing is not the lowest, is not what man has in common with the other animals, but rather what differentiates him, what makes him man: reason, and the self-command which enable him to subordinate his instincts to his formation as a truly conscious being, capable of free acts and constructive purpose.

Man is an animal able to act freely, that is to make choices. To choose demands a knowledge of what is good and of what is better. The love which is proper to human nature is not "instinctive" love, but one which is capable of choosing the good love worthy of man. And this good of a worthy love is what makes freedom and a constant aim possible. The nature of man does not demand to be abandoned to the rule of instinct but to choose and to remain constant in love. This is what the psychologists call a "difficult" mode of behaviour. But it is proper to the very nature of man to know and to be able to choose the "difficult" way and to advance along it without faltering, in spite of his falls.[3]

[3] In his excellent book *Le Trône de la sagesse*, Fr Bouyer writes that "St Augustine, in spite of his sincere efforts to defend the holiness of marriage, never managed it ... he could not think of it except as a kind of permitted or tolerated sin." And he continues, "What Augustine apparently could not see is that the root of evil, here, is not so much in the materiality of our nature as in the weakness of our will.... This is the error that St Thomas was to notice and avoid." The problem is a complex one: the human spirit is the form of a body. "It follows that, in concrete terms, it is useless to attempt, within the range of human sensibility, to isolate sensations and desires in a pure state from a will that is no longer pure. The impaired state of our will is revealed in the expression in concrete terms of desires and sensations which are, indissolubly, both spiritual and fleshly. Truly this is a wound to our entire nature, undivided, a wound to the body as well as to the spirit.... Habitual consent to the demands of desire, the acceptance of pleasure without reserve, will remain the path of sin and death" (p. 112).

THE PURPOSE OF MARRIAGE   **19**

Along this road which is proper to man lies the will and the power to pass something on: his experience and the lesson it teaches. Man is by nature able to record history, that is, to *remember*. So, first of all, he is able to pass on to a child, to his child, a knowledge of life which is not defined in words only.

Married union, one and indissoluble, destined for the education as well as the creation of children, and for the mutual fulfilment of the partners in this creation and education and the handing on of values that this implies, is, then, by an extension of instinct at an authentically human level, the true expression of human nature.

Dr Allers, among many others, has emphasized that the normal is not the same as the average. What is normal for man is not what was or is done by the average man. The normal thing for man is what corresponds to his nature as man, that is to the reason, the self-command, the will to pass on his values, of which we spoke.

Even though the average man, or the majority of men, would not be willing to accept the unity and indissolubility of the marriage bond, we could not conclude that man's love is normally multiple and inconstant. Man's nature is still defined by what man ought to be, by what he is called to be, and from this point of view also it is permanent union with one, and not the multiple appeal of "instinct", which truly expresses the deepest nature of man.

DON JUAN, OR DESIRE WITHOUT REMEDY

Nevertheless the myth of Don Juan, the eternal seeker after love, the lover ever unsatisfied, is still the expression of the painful—though many would call it glorious—state of man in love. This freedom of choice, this search for the one who will be the best complement to ourselves—it seems "natural" to recognize these things in the quest, constantly renewed, for another partner in love, and we find no contradiction in experience which shows us so many examples of such a quest, and with it the spectacle of lovers' hearts eternally unsatisfied.

Nothing can usefully be said about that incarnation of human love which we call marriage unless at the very beginning we consider the reality of this unsatisfied love. In this context the words of St Teresa of Avila stand out: "There is no remedy for our desire." But which love? And which desire?

There is but one love. It is the true expression of our nature, this leaping flame that feeds on any straw, this call whose reverberation fills our nights, our dark forests, with its cry. For we are what is never complete in itself, we are beings never satisfied with the nourishment offered us.

We seek in "another" what God alone can give us, and to many this search has seemed mad: on the one hand to those who do not know what love is and see in it only the need and the cry of the flesh, but on the other hand to those also who have built between the love of God and the love of creatures the impassable barrier of Manicheism or, worse still, of Jansenism.

But in truth for those who are not called to the high vocation of loving God alone, the way to the love of God is still to be found through the love of creatures.

"There are two precepts," says St Augustine, "but only one charity. The charity by which we love our neighbour is none other than the charity by which we love God. The love which impels us to love our neighbour is the same as that with which we love God."[4] And Dom Massabki writes: "There is no distinction to be made between the love of God and the love of men who are one body with the Son of God . . . our reason for loving God and our reason for loving our neighbour are the same."[5]

We love because we are not sufficient to ourselves. The man who turns in upon himself and lives for himself alone

[4] In Joan. 87.
[5] Dom Massabki, Le Sacrament de l'Amour.

does not love and is not loved. The true mystery of love lies in this, that in the leaving of self, to which act love impels us, we take in giving and are taken by our gift. We love because we are not sufficient to ourselves. What is it that we need?

We need to be more than ourselves, to enter into the great gesture of Creation which is inseparably both gift and love. Another being brings to us this extension of existence in the union of love. But how can there be union without common life? It is in this context that the words of Scripture take on their full meaning: they shall be *one flesh*. And not only in the flesh but in all that they are, in all their human being.

In the flesh, first of all, because a human being is woven from this flesh. It is the vessel and the sign, not the means only but the pledge and the place of that union.

We need this other being. Not just any other, but this particular other, and we shall see later the place that freedom of choice holds in the Christian conception of love. *We take* this other one. But how can a human being take another to himself unless by a violence which is itself inhuman? Only by a gift, a total gift, which can never be reclaimed.

So the need for permanence in marriage is rooted in the very heart of a human nature. You are entirely mine only if I am yours for always. But what I expect to receive from you is far more and far other than yourself, it is to take part with you, through your gift of self to me, in the unending process of the creation of being. So your body and mine are united not so much for their own sakes as for the sake of that need they have in common—the need to go further, to create. They can only do so together and neither will reach its goal unless all has been done together.

From the heart of this need for married union there springs another need, the need not only to serve each other, but to make that service fully effective in a common service of something else, a united gaze towards what alone can make us wholly what we should be, that is, towards the God whose plan we carry out by the creation of children who shall extend it into infinite futurity.

In this way, and in this way alone, the mystery of love is made plain, that love in which every gift is gain, every gain is a gift. And all gain which is not also a gift, and a total gift, becomes nothing more than capture by violence and the absolute negation of love.

At the same time it is clear that love which is for each other alone is not worthy of the name of love, for that only is love which is a common participation in the source from which the two lovers take their being. So the myth of Don Juan takes on a real meaning, and finds that meaning in the words of St Teresa already quoted: Don Juan is the man who imagines that he can satisfy his needs by the capture of another being: he hopes to gain from this finite being the satisfaction of an infinite need. At this level it is certainly true that "there is no remedy for our desire". For Don Juan's grasp closes on himself at the very moment when he thinks he has made the world his own. He becomes less in the very act by which he had thought to add to himself, he cuts himself off from the world by what should have given him entry to the heart of it. To violate the world is to murder it, for the world is a living secret, mystery itself.

Love which is shut in on itself, even between two, is a dike to shut out the world. Love which shares in the creative will of God opens the sluice-gates to the world. Certainly human love will never be satisfied with the bounds of our numbered days, for it is infinity that we demand; but the mutual gift in communion with the creative will of God holds open the floodgates through which foam the waves of the gift of love. It makes sure that we shall lie always open to the ever-renewed tides of grace that flow over us from the Father through the Son and the Holy Spirit.

Understanding this, we are led still further. In our age as in others there is no lack of writers and thinkers who would persuade us to refuse the gift of self precisely in order that we may remain open and available. But it seems on the contrary that it is by accepting the world in this gift of a love chosen and founded once for all that we are enabled to remain open to receive the flood that bears the contribution of the world.

It is the gift of self which makes me available for a creation that is ever new. To refuse it makes me null and sterile. The life of the flesh itself chalks up its great lesson: those who refuse the child and the natural development of love will know no future. In their death they will die.

THE FLESH IS MUCH MORE THAN THE FLESH

In these latter years there has been much talk about sex and sexuality, of the need to understand and respect them. It is necessary to do so. But we are talking about sex in human beings.

There has been a curious development in the thought on this subject. Not long ago we were being told to see things as they really are, to be rid of deceptive idealism. True enough, man's gaze demands the truth. But the next generation interpreted this *realism* as *materialism*, and drew from it conclusions quite different from those promised. "Your body is your own," muttered the popular voice, "it is only a body." Therefore there arose two great cries of revolt. One, which attempted to live entirely by this materialism, was a cry of despair: if life, if love itself, is nothing but that, it is all folly, "man is a useless passion", it is impossible to touch another being, even in love.

But another cry re-echoes in our age, philosophers and psychologists discover a *meaning* in each important act of our lives, and for them the sexual act is the first to be thus charged with meaning. This idea has reappeared, oddly enough, in the recently published correspondence of that great purifier of sex, Sigmund Freud.

This sexual act that men had thought to reduce to the

category of a purely physiological reflex was revealed by psycho-analysis as something infinitely charged with "meaning". It is not true that the sexual act can be separated from all that precedes it in the mind and all that follows it in living. Right was on the side neither of those who thought to rid themselves of it by regarding it as shameful and hidden nor of those who believed they could free it from its "complexes" purely and simply by "liberating" it, by handing it over to what they imagined was itself, to its naked materiality, to its bare skeleton.[6]

But men, doctrinaire materialists or, more often, men of science, who tried to reduce the sexual act to a purely physiological reflex, discovered at the very heart of their analysis the link which bound it to the whole psyche, they found that from thence it sprang and then in its turn dominated the whole future development of the human being. At the very moment when it seemed possible to say with assurance that sexuality was a material act of no importance, as void of meaning as "drinking a glass of water when one is thirsty"

---

[6] We may recall here the passage from Fr Bouyer quoted in the footnote on page 18. He also says: "What was spoiled by original sin was not some outlying province of our sensibility. As the great prophets said, it was the heart. That is, it was our will, at the point at which it bears on instinct and should rule it. The more intimate an impulse is, and the more deeply rooted in our nature, the holier it was in its origin. In fact there is no doubt that in its practical application it runs all the greater risk of being a perpetual occasion of falls for us, and so must become the occasion of perpetual renunciation and sacrifice. From this point of view, all Christians, whether living and using marriage or consecrated to God as virgins, can find once more a human meaning in sexuality. It is certainly capable of positive fulfilment. But that does not mean that it will cease to be a reason for sacrifice as much as ever. On the contrary, the more it is recognized as the central theme of human life, the more apparent it will be that it can be an obstacle for us in the way of salvation. If it is our very life that we must renounce, so that we may save it as the Gospel teaches us, the fact that we have restored to its full dignity in our natural life one particular sphere of our desires and joys does not mean that we can withdraw it from the need for sacrifice. Rather is it marked out for sacrifice" (*Trône de la sagesse*, p. 113).

as people used to say around 1900, it was among the most "scientific" of the analysts of sexual activity that there arose the evidence of its deep meaning. It was rediscovered by the admittedly strange ways of Freudianism, but the discoveries were major ones: that there are strong links between sexuality and the highest functions of the soul; that the act of love was, or was not, beneficial to the whole being in so far as it was performed with joy and full consent or without the heart's approval; that the normality or otherwise of sexual activity affected the entire psyche.

Our brother the flesh was no longer a separated brother. He had regained his place in the harmony of the being as a whole. And whatever destroyed its balance at the same time endangered the balance of the soul. Some people persuaded themselves that materialism had gained another victory, made a new conquest, that the body had made a further advance at the expense of the soul. Not at all: the results of the work of psychologists and even of physiologists were to show that the unbalance of the soul had an even greater effect on the body than that of the body on the soul, so that finally it was the traditional position of Christian psychology that was verified, that which Fr Sertillanges, in his great book on St Thomas Aquinas, described thus: "The fundamental principle of Thomist psychology, that boldly, brilliantly and providentially (considering the future of science) renewed the principle of Aristotelian psychology, is that the human soul can only be completely defined in relation to the body which it animates and with which it forms a true and substantial unity."[7]

The twentieth century has no time for that ignorance of the body which the nineteenth century called "idealism" and which combined so oddly with a transparent hypocrisy. But neither will it accept any doctrine of absolute materialism in sexuality.

[7] *Saint Thomas d'Aquin*, 2, p. 159.

MARRIED UNION IS NECESSARY IN ORDER TO BECOME AN INTEGRATED HUMAN BEING

The rediscovery of the meaning of sexual life has become not only possible but easy. And at the same time it has become evident once more that when human personality is considered in its total harmony marriage lies at its very root.

So that in this second half of the twentieth century more than ever is it possible and necessary to affirm that the sexual morality taught by Christianity is not a morality of Christianity but the morality of nature as God willed it to be. And more than ever is it possible and necessary to show that marriage is the key to that morality and the expression of that nature. Union in marriage is not against nature. It is the expression of that nature, conceived as a unity of body and spirit, such as the wisest philosophers had instinctively felt it must be and as twentieth-century physiology had confirmed it to be. Married union is not contrary to instinct. As Abbé Monchanin has excellently put it: "The normal instinct is one which has completely fulfilled its purpose" and since, according to another concise definition by the same author, "instinct, even when it is strongly localized, gives a unity of direction to the whole man", unity of love in the unity of marriage seems to be exactly what is needed for the integration of a personality.

And the same author, showing that the Christian idea of marriage is concerned "neither to refuse nor to revile instinct" sums up in this way: "Whoever breaks the bond of monogamous marriage, either temporarily or for good, dissociates his instincts from his life by seeking immediate sexual satisfaction while refusing to recognize its influence on the psyche."

It is therefore both possible and necessary, today more than ever, to state that, after considering all the results of research

in psycho-physiology and psycho-analysis, the Christian conception of a single and monogamous marriage fulfils the
deepest needs of human nature.[8]

THE MARRIED COUPLE SHARE IN THE WORKING
OUT OF GOD'S PLAN

To say that a single monogamous marriage is in conformity
with the nature of things as willed by God, requires us to
examine more closely both that nature itself and the divine
will.

The whole of natural life was created by God for his glory
and tends to glorify him. Married union, the root of man's
existence on earth and the basis of his life on that earth, takes
first place in the ordering of creatures for the glory of God.
When, through their flesh, husband and wife create what will
be the flesh of the future, the future people of God, they are
directly obeying God's creative will, they are following it,
making it real and effective.

The whole of this nature is also a symbol, an expression,
of God's life. The whole of nature proclaims his glory:
enarrant coeli gloriam. Married union, from which springs the
life of man, incarnates the symbol of divine life in a special
way.

Those Christian authors who have recently written about
marriage are wont to do more than compare the union of
Christ and the Church with that of bride and bridegroom;
they establish a real parallel between the two.

Dom Massabki writes: "The union of Christ and the Church
is the most intimate and complete union that is possible. On
the cross, Christ freely made a total gift of his bodily life to
the Church."[9] In the Eucharist he gave himself to her
entirely. The Church for her part gives herself so completely

[8] Obviously we are here leaving out of consideration those vocations
to asceticism and chastity which receive their grace by a different gift.
[9] We shall see later that the Church makes of this freedom in giving
an essential condition of the validity of marriage.

to Christ in loving surrender that she forms but one whole with him as the body is one with the head. Conformed to Christ and to the Church, bride and bridegroom must attempt to realize an analogous union, to give themselves with the same completeness, the same perfection." And Dom Massabki quotes St Paul (Ephes. 5. 22–4): "Wives must obey their husbands as they would obey the Lord. The man is the head to which the woman's body is united, just as Christ is the head of the Church, he, the Saviour on whom the safety of his body depends; and women must owe obedience in all points to their husbands, as the Church does to Christ."

Can we conclude from a text such as this that an absolute parallel exists between the relation of husband and wife and the relation of Christ and the Church? There is no question of this, and the reasons are obvious, the first one being in the very nature of a relationship between creatures and the fact that it is realized through the senses, physically, even though it is rooted deeper and grows higher. Yet St Paul himself goes further, saying that the bride is the completion of the bridegroom as Christ is completed by the Church which "is his body, the completion of him who in all things is complete" (Ephes. 1. 23). And again: "You who are husbands must show love to your wives, as Christ showed love to the Church when he gave himself up on its behalf" (Ephes. 5. 25). We can see more clearly here the meaning that we should learn from this symbol. It is the greatness of an absolute giving which is here envisaged.

There is a mystery of the union of husband and wife, as there is a mystery of the unity of Christ and the Church. It is a good thing to seek in this analogy light by which to deepen our understanding of the mystery of marriage, and it helps us to see more clearly the spiritual nature of that mystery. But between that which is of creatures, imperfect as they are at their very root, and that which belongs to the mystery of God, seen in its essential gift, its most intimate communication through the sacrifice of the Son, there is a gulf which imagination must not attempt to cross.[10]

But the fact remains that again and again Scripture uses the image of the Bride in order to describe the Church: "I have betrothed you to Christ, so that no other than he should claim you, his bride without spot", writes St Paul (2 Cor. 11. 2), and such texts could be multiplied, together with later ones from St John of the Cross and many other mystics. Certainly there is in all this a reminder to us not to forget the high dignity of the bodily act as the means of handing on created life. It gives to the sexual act its rightful place as an essential part of the realization of God's plan for the world.

In the same way that Christ, in and for the Church which is his body, obtains and restores supernatural life, so the husband, in and by the wife, obtains the renewal of natural life. We must not forget the differences: this life is not his, the husband's, whereas the life of the Church comes from the Father who is one with the Son—and also directly from the Son; on the other hand the wife is the vessel only of a nature still in need and expectation of being saved.

If in exalting the dignity of married life we forget none of these limits and differences then we shall be able to exalt it without fear, for we are now in a better position than before to measure its height. We have seen the greatness of married life in its participation, secondary but none the less real, in the continuation of God's creation in the order of nature. What we have to consider now is an even higher dignity.

[10] Dom Massabki writes: "Perfect chastity is a better figure of the union of Christ and the Church, for there the union is entirely spiritual. Christian marriage symbolizes this union through the medium of material reality, that is, in the union of the flesh. . . ." But then we find these words from the pen of Pius VIII (*Traditi humilitati*): "But it is in fact certain that the union in marriage, *whose author is God, represents* the perpetual and exalted union of Christ the Saviour and the Church, and that this close community of man and wife is the sacrament, that is to say, the holy sign of the immortal love of Christ for his Bride."

Husband and wife do not create a merely natural thing. It is impossible to separate natural and supernatural in this creation. Hence we find that husband and wife take part indirectly in the great drama of divine adoption and of redemption. When the popes (Pius VIII for example, in the encyclical *Traditi humilitati*) speak of the holiness of marriage and say that it should be "numbered among things sacred" they do not speak lightly nor merely symbolically. What they mean is that in the design of creation itself the mission of husband and wife is part of the work which is to lead the procession of humanity towards its goal.

MARRIAGE IS A SACRAMENT BECAUSE IT IS ALSO A SACRED ACT

Replying to the "naturalist philosophers", Leo XIII wrote these important lines: "Since the institution of marriage is from God himself, and since from the beginning marriage has been as it were the image of the Incarnation of the Word, it follows that there is a sacred and religious quality in marriage, a quality not added on but innate, coming not from man but from nature itself" (Encyclical *Arcanum*). It is not the sacrament which makes marriage holy. It is holy and therefore it is a sacrament. Leo XIII recalls that Innocent III and Honorius III "felt able to affirm without rashness and with good reason that the sacrament of marriage exists among both believers and unbelievers". What he means is that the act of marriage itself is holy as a fact of nature willed by God. The sacrament does not add something to it, it is the recognition of, the witness to, this sacred quality in marriage.

Pius XI emphasized this: "The light of reason alone—above all if we study the ancient records of history, if we question the unchanging conscience of peoples, if we examine the institutions and moral codes of nations—is enough to establish that there is in marriage itself a sacred and religious quality" (Encyclical *Casti Connubii*). And after quoting the passage from Leo XIII given above Pius XI continues: "The sacred character of marriage, intimately linked to the order of religion and of holy things, is the effective result of its divine origin and also of its purpose which is to bring children to birth and to form them for God, and at the same time to bind husband and wife to God in Christian love and mutual help; and finally it is the result of the duty which is natural to married union itself, instituted as it is by the all-wise Providence of God the Creator, the duty to serve as a sort of medium for the transmission of life, by which parents become as it were the instruments of the almighty power of God." To emphasize still further that the sacred character of marriage is inherent in its nature Pius XII reminds us that "even among those who are not baptized, legitimately con-tracted marriage is, in the natural order, a sacred thing".[11] Marriage, then, which receives its sacred character equally from its origin, purpose and laws, and from the union of Christ and the Church which it symbolizes, is as it were a sacrament by nature.

Contrary to the way we often think of it, the sacrament is not just something that is added on from outside—by the Church for example—to the natural character of marriage. Marriage is sacred in itself: that is what we mean when we say, and truly, that the bride and groom administer the sacra-ment of marriage to each other, while the priest is there simply to bear witness to its existence.[12] But it would be entirely contrary to the mind of the Church to exalt the rôle of the contracting parties too much: what they do is simply to

[11] Allocution to the tribunal of the Rota, charged with matrimonial cases (October 6th, 1946).

[12] Cf. especially: Leo XIII: "In Christian marriage the contract can-not be dissociated from the sacrament ... every legitimate marriage is a sacrament by its very nature." Pius XII: "It is you yourselves whom God has appointed ministers of the sacrament" (Address to young couples).

acknowledge and confirm the order of nature to which they submit themselves.

Much could be said about the meaning of this. Whether consciously or not, the Christian of today gets into the habit of feeling—and then of arguing—that supernatural and sacramental reality are something extra, added from without to natural life and actions which could get on quite well by themselves. This creates an artificial gulf between natural and supernatural ignoring the close bond that in reality unites them, and so the idea takes root that there can be such a thing as an independent natural reality.

Quite the contrary; the supernatural is present at the very heart of nature; without it, nature ceases to be human nature since everything that is exists only by the creative will of God and depends on him for its continued existence.

This is verified, at a moment of especial importance in the life of man, by the sacred character of marriage itself. Together with the whole of life on earth, and especially in this that binds our life together, "the work of the Creator from the world's beginning, the union of man and woman was restored by Christ and integrated into the supernatural order of salvation".[13]

"Of divine institution, endowed by God with sacred and unchangeable duties ... (marriage) has been still further ennobled by Christ and raised to the dignity of a sacrament of the new law."[14]

THE ENDS OF CHRISTIAN MARRIAGE AND HUMAN DIGNITY IN MARRIED UNION

The two ends of marriage are linked

Much discussion has centred on the question of the "ends" of marriage: what is its essential purpose? Or rather, what was it designed for? *Why* does it exist? In the light of what

[13] Dom Boissard, *Questions théologiques sur le mariage.*
[14] *Ibid.*

we have considered above about its essence, its nature, of the way in which it is the expression of human nature itself as it is ordered according to the divine plan for the world, there appears to be little room for hesitation. Recent pontifical texts leave no room for doubt on this point. One in particular, already quoted above, provides us with an absolutely unequivocal summary of Catholic thought on the ends of marriage.

Pius XI wrote in *Casti Connubii*: "The sacred character of marriage, intimately linked to the order of religion and of holy things, is the effective result of its divine origin ... and also of its purpose which is to bring children to birth and to form them for God, and at the same time to bind husband and wife to God in Christian love and mutual help; and finally, it is the result of the duty which is natural to married union itself, instituted as it is by the all-wise Providence of God the Creator, the duty to serve as a sort of medium for the transmission of life, by which parents become as it were the instruments of the almighty power of God."

What we call the two ends of married union stand out clearly here: the handing on of life and what is sometimes called the "fulfilment" of two people in the community of Christian life. But we can also see how, deeper down, these two ends are intimately linked: it is not primarily a question of bringing children to birth but of bringing children to birth and forming them for God; and the fulfilment of these two human persons is the direct result of binding them to God *at the same time* "in Christian love and mutual help"; finally, "the duty which is natural to married union" is described as the handing on of life "by which parents become as it were the instruments of the almighty power of God", which shows clearly that their mission of handing on life is inseparable from their own Christian life, from their incorporation in the mystical Body of Christ, without which they would have neither the dignity nor the grace, nor even the special kind of life which enables them to be truly the "instruments of the almighty power of God".

All this becomes quite clear in the light of what has been said above about the inseparability of natural and super-natural activity.

Procreation the primary end, emphasized by the Old Testament

But the controversy, now settled, which centred on the problem of the "ends" of marriage, was chiefly concerned with the relationship between, the relative importance of, the two ends: the birth of children and the mutual help the couple give each other in achieving their own personal "fulfilment" in love.

The passage in Genesis relating the creation of man and woman first gives procreation as the only end: "Man and woman both he created them" and he said to them, "Increase and multiply and fill the earth" (Gen. 1. 28). But immediately afterwards there follows a more detailed account. God made woman because "it is not well that man should be without companionship; I will give him a mate of his own kind" (Gen. 2. 18). Fr Lavaud in a study of "the divine plan for marriage"[15] recalls that Fr Lagrange translates "of his own kind" by "an opposite number" and Fr Hummelauer explains that he means a being who corresponds and is proportioned to himself.

After this second account comes the following passage: "That is why a man is destined to leave his father and mother and cling to his wife instead, so that the two become one flesh." And Fr Lavaud comments as follows: "That is, the marriage bond contracted by these two people is in some respects closer and stronger than the natural bond between parents and children. Here the first and indeed the only con-sideration is this fusion of two lives into one new entity, distinct from those out of which sprang the husband and

[15] *Etudes Carmélitaines*: "L'Esprit et la Vie" (April, 1938).

wife, the closeness of this act of union. 'So that the two become one flesh' is sometimes taken to refer to the fruit of union, the child, in whom the parents rediscover each other, but this interpretation of its meaning is clearly only an indirect and secondary one. The inspired author is considering primarily the community of man and woman, a community which by God's blessing will grow into a family."[16]

The idea of married union that is dominant in the Old Testament is that of fecundity. Women are considered blessed when they are fruitful. After their captivity in Egypt Yahweh promises his people, in return for their service, "to enrich thee with the bread and water thou needest, and keep sickness far away from thy company; there shall be no unfruitfulness in thy land, no barrenness" (Exod. 23. 25). The Psalms also proclaim the blessing of fecundity: "Fatherhood itself is the Lord's gift, the fruitful womb is a reward that comes from him, Crown of thy youth, children are like arrows in a warrior's hand. Happy whose quiver is well filled with these" (Ps. 126. 2–4).

When the angel explains to Tobias how he should behave towards his bride, "with the fear of the Lord upon thee", he bids him take the girl "moved rather by the hope of begetting children than by any lust of thine" (Tob. 6. 22). But even in the book of Tobias there is already a delicacy in the description of the mutual love of bride and bridegroom which holds promise of a different view.

That view emerges substantially from the New Testament. Jesus gave to the commandment "thou shalt not covet thy neighbour's wife" an entirely new meaning which is indicated by these words: "You have heard that it was said, Thou shalt not commit adultery. But I tell you that he who casts his eyes on a woman so as to lust after her has already committed adultery with her in his heart" (Matt. 5. 27). He was substituting a complete morality of intention and of respect towards the human person for the morality of external

[16] *Ibid.*

conformity. Here, as in the whole of the New Testament, a purely social system of ethics is superseded by the ethics of personal conduct. Married union is no longer to be guarded simply because it brings children to birth, but for its own sake; it is the relationship with another person (even when it does not issue in action) which is sacred.

The end of "mutual help" is made clear in the New Testament

In the same spirit St Paul condemns lust in the name of respect for the human body: "But your bodies are not meant for debauchery, they are meant for the Lord, and the Lord claims your bodies. . . . Have you ever been told that your bodies belong to the body of Christ? . . . the fornicator is committing a sin against his own body. Surely you know that your bodies are the shrines of the Holy Spirit . . . so that you are no longer your own masters. A great price was paid to ransom you; glorify God by making your bodies the shrines of his presence" (1 Cor. 6. 13–20).

Fr Lavaud comments on these passages: "St Paul reproves fornication and other forms of licentiousness, not so much in terms of the natural order of which standard doctrine would have made use (since the blessing of a child may spring from forbidden love, and debauchery may end in sterility) but rather because sexual intercourse, which fuses two bodies into one flesh, is so complete a gift that it can only be permitted to couples who legitimately belong to each other for always. If the surrender of the body each to the other is not the result of a simultaneous gift of the soul it is a degradation of both the one and the other." [17]

We are here in a world in which the human being has taken on an appearance that emerged far more faintly in the Old Testament. The whole of Christian thought was to concern itself with making it clearer still. The early Fathers of the Church (whether because they were still close to the old Law

---

[17] *Etudes Carmélitaines*: "L'Esprit et la Vie," p. 189.

or, as Fr Lavaud has suggested, because they were convinced that the end of the world was near) either, like St Clement, considered procreation as the only end or, like Tertullian and Origen, thought of marriage chiefly as a cure for concupiscence. But with St Basil and St Gregory of Nyssa there appeared the idea of mutual help. St John Chrysostom saw in it one of the means to Christian perfection.[18]

In St Augustine's mind the procreation of children was the "sole reason for the creation of woman"; but from the time of Eve's birth, and because she was destined to complete man, their association is natural and good in itself. But St Augustine always sees the act of procreation, even in marriage, as linked with concupiscence and therefore with evil.

The Thomist analysis shows that the sexual act is good in itself

At this point St Thomas Aquinas throws on the question the light of his profound analysis of human action. He saw that if an act is good (as in the case of marriage) the pleasure with which it is linked could not be a sin. A human action performed in the normal way and in submission to its normal ends cannot be sinful.

So it is St Thomas who reveals for the first time that complete view of marriage which has been the constant teaching of the Church, and which presents the procreation of children as the first and primary end of married union, and next to it the love and mutual help of husband and wife or, as our contemporaries might prefer to put it, their mutual fulfilment.

Two schools of thought are to be found among modern theologians and moralists. One regards the mutual fulfilment of the couple as the essential purpose of married union, and puts procreation in the second place. The other reverses the order, putting procreation in the first place. We shall see later how these two tendencies have been envisaged by the Church;

[18] An excellent synthesis of the position of the Fathers of the Church is contained in the article, already quoted, by Fr Lavaud, based on *The Ends of Christian Marriage* by J. E. Marr, O.P.

she has singled out the procreation of children as the primary end. But for all that, this exchange of views has certainly enriched and deepened the Christian idea of marriage. The importance of this discussion both in itself and for the sake of the interest it has aroused in the modern world, makes it desirable to examine it in rather more detail.

In the opinion of Dom Boissard the immediate end, that is the one first achieved, "is to give the couple, through the close, complete and final union of the lover's person with that of the beloved, that completion which is his natural desire: a deeply valued support—material, bodily, sensual, emotional and spiritual all at the same time—which is for the majority of human beings the providential means to their personal and social perfection, of their moral progress and of their sanctification".[19]

This is that first end which theologians call mutual help and which is nowadays often called the completion or fulfilment of the husband and wife. "These words," says Dom Boissard, "are strong evidence of that first impression that love—and the marriage act which is its expression—brings in its train: the feeling of having suddenly acquired a new dimension of being which transforms life, renewing in the lovers their vision of the world and of themselves, a feeling that an empty space has been filled. From this spring important consequences, at once moral, intellectual, religious and supernatural."[20]

Dom Boissard maintains that these effects of marriage make it permissible to use expressions such as the *completion* or *fulfilment* of the partners. At the same time he believes that it is better to speak of the "perfection" of husband and wife, and that for two reasons; firstly because this term does not reduce the magnitude of the transformation which takes place to an effect produced once for all at the outset of the marriage, and secondly because the word "perfection" has moral and

[19] Dom Boissard, *Questions théologiques sur le mariage*, p. 17.
[20] *Ibid.*

spiritual overtones which are lacking in the words "completion" and "fulfilment".

We are in agreement with Dom Boissard on all these points and we shall go even further: because there can be neither completion nor fulfilment for human beings in this life, the stage which is marked by union in marriage is not the end—it opens the door to further experience, it leads on to other possibilities. And in particular we shall see that there is a ceaseless give and take between this end and that of the procreation of children, a constantly renewed relationship: the union of the partners leads to the birth of children, but the children lead their parents (often through agony and tears) to a new stage in their union, even though the parents may not recognize it at the time.

The twofold means of the perfection of the couple

We cannot entirely agree with Dom Boissard when he writes that this end of personal fulfilment "is chiefly an individual matter". Although he explains that the perfection of the married couple "has besides a considerable social value" still he leaves the impression that there is a division between personal and social life. But in fact, as we have seen, the perfection of husband and wife in their common life is not wrought solely by the direct exchange of love, but also and above all by their common involvement in life itself, an involvement which includes the birth and education of the children, the acceptance by each of the other's shortcomings, their shouldering together of certain forms of work for the community. Hence it is through the whole of family and social life that the couple work towards perfection, and from this springs the two-sided concept which is essential to our argument: the individual is always orientated towards the City in which he finds himself; the person as such is orientated towards God; hence, that neither the most completely material individuality nor the most completely spiritual personality may, in their search for perfection, be deprived of their involvement in the world.

After noting that the end of marriage which is procreation ("and the education that must follow") is social and even universal since what it seeks is "the perpetuation of the race, the increase of the natural human society and of the mystical City of God", Dom Boissard adds most pertinently that all this "contributes notably to the personal perfection of the partners, for the birth and education of the children draws them and binds them together with new bonds, prolongs and develops in time their wonderful participation in the fruitfulness of the divine persons". And he adds something that leads to the essential part, the crux of the whole problem: "Between these two ends there is no contradiction, rather they are complementary, each is involved in the other: in seeking their own and each other's fulfilment and perfection the couple contribute effectively to the well-being of the whole of society; and on the other hand the birth and education of their offspring is not only profitable to both Church and State, but is also the fulfilment of the parents' deepest desires, for in a sense these extend their being and their union beyond the limits of our earthly life, bringing increase of merit and new strength to married love (or, as we would prefer to put it, making a radical transformation in its very essence) by saving it from the danger of a shared egoism."[21]

The end of the partners' perfection is secondary in relation to the end of creation within God's plan for the world.

In the end, then, Dom Boissard is forced to ask the question which is unavoidable at this point in the discussion: Must we rest content with this duality of ends? He concludes that they have a proper order:

> If the immediate end—the desire to give oneself to the beloved for life, to receive the gift of love in return, to seek in that union joy, strength and spiritual progress—is the one

[21] *Questions théologiques sur le mariage*, p. 19.

which takes first place in the minds of the engaged couples and is frequently psychologically dominant (especially in the man),[22] the fact remains nonetheless that a virtually unanimous Christian tradition places the procreation and education of children for God as the end highest in dignity. Theologians and canonists, following in the footsteps of the Fathers, have always regarded this as the first and principal end of marriage, "the most essential end" as St Thomas says, without which it can be neither understood nor defined.[23]

Dom Massabki, already quoted, and many other modern authors who would go much further in the same direction,[24] seem to regard the end of the full development of husband and wife as definitely the primary one. Dom Massabki quotes this essential passage from Pius XI's encyclical *Casti Connubii*:

In the community of the home love is not expressed by mutual support only: it must aim higher, in fact its principal objective must be to strive every day to form and perfect the interior life each in the other. Their day-to-day relationship will help them to make daily progress in virtue, above all to grow in true charity towards God and their neighbour, that charity in which all the Law and the Prophets are finally summed up. . . . This growth of the interior life of the couple, this continual effort to help each other towards perfection, can even, and truly, be called the cause and primary reason of marriage as the Roman catechism teaches,[25] at least if we do not look at marriage as strictly an institution intended for the procreation and education of children, but take a wider view of it as the sharing of life as a whole, an habitual intimacy— a society.

Can there be opposition or disagreement between this teaching of Pius XI in *Casti Connubii* and the decree of the

[22] This seems to us less certain.

[23] *Op. cit.*, p. 20.

[24] Doms, for instance. Dom Massabki makes use of more or less the same ideas as Dom Boissard but looks at them from a different point of view.

[25] Qu. 2, Ch. 8.

Holy Office of April 1st, 1944, which seemed to have ended these skirmishings by a definite ruling? This is in fact mentioned in the decree itself, after a summary of the various opinions presented: "Can we entertain the opinion of some modern authorities who deny that the primary end of marriage is procreation and education, or teach that the secondary ends are not necessarily subordinate to the primary one but are equally important and independent? The members of the Sacred Congregation of the Holy Office have decided to reply in the negative." This reply was approved by Pius XII on March 30th, 1944. A sufficiently careful examination of the two Roman texts quoted here shows that there is no opposition between them.

Is it in fact possible in psychological terms to say with conviction that the couple will provide for each other all that they need to fill the horizon of their lives? For reasons in which psychology and metaphysics complement each other it is quite clear that this is not the case. Once again the quotation from St Teresa of Avila comes to mind: "There is no remedy for our desire." No human reality, no human love even, can crown our hope, can be our fulfilment except a love sufficiently deep, sufficiently detached from the other as well as from self to be able to share a conviction that neither is enough to fill the whole of the world's horizons, whence it follows that in order to make a full response to the other each must make a complete surrender, a gift involving everything in oneself which transcends the self, so making this transcendence the common goal.

Fulfilment and perfection by transcendence in creation through love

Romantic love came near to perceiving this, but concluded that the lover must sacrifice to the beloved even what belongs to his inmost being, even God. But in fact as, and in so far as, he makes such a "sacrifice" the lover empties himself of what is most essential to him and becomes incapable of making the response awaited by the beloved. But when, recognizing his insufficiency, he seeks to give more than himself, and with the beloved to project into the future the fruits of a love which by that very fact is without end, then, and only then, does human love become truly worthy of man, of a being *capax Dei*, capable of reaching out to God and loving him.

In other words, in the measure in which lover and beloved turn in upon themselves, by just so much do they cease to be able to respond to each other's needs. This closing in on themselves withers them, they become in some way dried up and unfruitful.

Any psychology worthy of human beings acknowledges that there can be no fulfilment or flowering of the whole human being save through his integration into the great universal reality of fruitfulness through the centuries of which God is at once source, key and witness. Even in the depths of love itself the two human beings do not fulfil themselves except by adventuring themselves into that future which already lives in them in the moment in which they breed it.

It is easy to see from this how and why we must reject (as the 1944 Decree of the Holy Office demands) the idea of raising the fulfilment and development of husband and wife to the position of the "principal and independent" end of marriage. A "fulfilment" which is shut in on itself leads not only to withering and sterility (sterility in oneself, even sterility of love) but thence to despair, either in the "romantic" form of the suppression of new life, or in the "existentialist" form which, concluding that "man is a useless passion" or that "life is absurd", simply acts on the assumption that life, even with love, even shared between two, is self-enclosed and fruitless.

But all this is quite in line with *Casti Connubii* and in particular with the passage quoted above.

Those who may have been shocked by the idea that, in and through love, the end of the human creature is the "species" have in fact missed the point under discussion here. It is they who lack a sufficient sense of human dignity.

The human species is not, like animal species, a series of individuals constantly repeated. It is a slow ascension, a story of redemption "through the application of the merits of our Lord". To beget is not simply to beget in the flesh, it does not mean only to create new individuals but to create new *persons*, that is, beings who will follow us in the unending quest for God.

"In their struggle towards personal perfection," writes Dom Boissard, "the couple will learn to love and to desire, in the marriage act itself, their service of the race and the City, the development of Christ's mystery and the design of Providence for all creation, far surpassing their own personal happiness in grandeur and importance." Certainly, between the two, the Christian has an entirely different conception of "happiness". He knows—unconsciously perhaps, but love eternally unsatisfied is providentially there to remind him of it, both in the psychological and the metaphysical context— he knows that in fact his true happiness lies and can only lie in creating with his beloved the wonder of a new cell of life. It reaches out into the future, it grasps the future, it is truly a conquering march on the future. And one of the poles of the mystery of love, closely linked to that march of mankind towards the great final conclusion, is the fact that love is aware of this call of life, a call to "the eternal and blessed life of souls destined for divine adoption".

At this point free will comes into the picture. We shall see this in the next chapter.

What we want to make clear is that if the analysis of the *ends* of marriage is carried out with sufficient thoroughness, that is, if it is extended to the level of the analysis of the *beings* in whom the vocation of marriage is realized, there is no longer any distinction between the *meaning* and *the ends* of marriage. Here, as in many other fundamental problems, it was because the being in question was insufficiently examined that it seemed necessary to add to the quest for the *ends* a quest for the *meaning* of life.

CHAPTER II

THE LAWS OF CHRISTIAN MARRIAGE AND MARRIED LIFE

THE LAWS OF CHRISTIAN MARRIAGE ARE DIVINE

"He's had his marriage dissolved in Rome." This phrase, often heard, shows not only a misunderstanding of the (rare) case when the marriage tribunal recognizes nullity (that is the non-existence of the marriage bond), but also ignorance of the nature of the bond itself. And this ignorance extends not only to Christian marriage but also to plain and simple marriage of which Christian marriage itself is only the recognition.

If it is true—as we hope to have shown—that this unique and indissoluble union of two beings is the voice in them of the deep desire of human nature to go to the limit in its need to continue through the centuries, if this is true then marriage is not something that is applied *from outside* by some institution or other, legal or even ecclesiastical, to the union of the two who have made this decision. It is itself the union of two beings, two who both know and will the conditions of their union and their unity.

This is the whole meaning of the "yes" that bride and bridegroom pronounce. This "yes" is not said only to the person standing at one's side, the chosen partner. It is a "yes" to the will of God made manifest in nature. It is consent at the deepest level to human nature as willed by God: "Yes, I consent to be what I must be as a creature destined to obey God's will on earth and to make it obeyed; yes, I consent to be what I must be, to my state as man or woman for better or for worse, in its need and in its glory, in its suffering and in its joy."

In *Casti Connubii* Pius XI repeats and makes his own the words of Leo XIII's *Arcanum* so as to emphasize the permanence of Christian teaching on marriage:

> Let us remember first the foundation which must remain intact and inviolate: marriage was neither instituted nor restored by man, but by God: nor was it by men but by the author of our nature himself, Christ our Lord, that marriage was *given its laws*, elevated and confirmed. It follows that these laws do not in any way depend on human will, or on any contrary agreement between the partners themselves. This is the doctrine of Scripture,[1] this is the constant tradition of the universal Church, this is the solemn definition of the Council of Trent which, borrowing the words of Holy Scripture itself, teaches and confirms that the perpetual indissolubility of marriage, its unity and unchangeableness, spring from God who is its author.[2]

So the laws of marriage are enacted neither by human legislation nor by the arbitrary will of the partners: marriage is unique, unchanging and indissoluble because in creating nature God willed that it should be so, and so created human nature that it is fittingly bound by these laws. So it is not the Church who *makes* marriage, neither does she *add* anything (except perhaps an extra dignity and grandeur) in making it a sacrament: it is the couple's "yes", it is their consent, that makes the marriage and which *is* the sacrament to which God is simply a witness through the priest who represents the Church.

---

[1] Gen. 2. 22, 23; Matt. 19. 3 and following; Ephes. 5. 23; see above, Chapter I.
[2] Council of Trent, Session 29.

THE PARTNERS MAKE THEIR MARRIAGE BY THEIR FREE CONSENT TO THESE LAWS

"Although by its very nature marriage is of divine institution, human will none the less has its part, a truly noble part, to play, for each particular marriage, in that it constitutes the union in marriage of a particular man and woman, has no other origin than the free consent of the couple."

No idea of marriage has ever appeared in the world, none can be imagined, which gives greater importance to human freedom since it is that freedom and that alone which, by accepting or refusing the deepest demands of human nature, creates its own bond and shoulders its own obligation. It is this freedom which makes the contract and its laws. The Church refuses, and has always refused, to recognize any validity in civil law which either opposes the idea of marriage which she teaches, or even confirms or adopts that idea, if at the same time it claims that marriage springs from such an act of legislation. She refuses in order to protect not the law of the Church only but the dignity of a human promise, of a free response to the call of God which is present in the very nature of man.

In a passage we have already quoted Pius XI in *Casti Connubii* repeats the words of Leo XIII in *Arcanum:* "The light of reason alone," he writes, "is sufficient to establish the fact that there is a sacred and religious quality in marriage which is not adventitious but innate, not bestowed by men but forming a natural part of marriage whose author is God and which has been from the beginning as it were an image of the Incarnation of God's word." People have spoken, and still speak, very lightly of the sacrament of marriage. It has been seen as an addition to the promises of bride and groom, or the nuptial blessing—sometimes even the Mass—has been taken for the sacrament. These errors, already current in his time, were refuted by Pius IX. He wrote as follows in his letter

Ad Apostolicae Sedis condemning the book by John Nepo-
mucene Nuytz on Canon Law: "Several errors concerning
marriage are also put forward: that it cannot be reasonably
shown that Jesus Christ raised marriage to the dignity of a
sacrament; that the sacrament of marriage is purely accessory
to the contract and may therefore be separated from it, and
that the sacrament itself consists of the nuptial blessing alone;
that the marriage bond is not indissoluble in natural law; that
the Church has no right to lay down diriment impediments,
but that this right belongs to the State, which alone has the
power to remove existing impediments; that matrimonial cases
and betrothals are naturally the affair of a civil tribunal; that
the Church, in the course of centuries, began to introduce
diriment impediments, not by any right that was properly hers,
but by a prerogative which she held from the State."

In setting out this catalogue of errors concerning marriage
in the middle of the nineteenth century, which, after the
profligacy of the eighteenth, had in its early years already tried
to subordinate religion to the State, the Church was pointing
out some directions in which the idea of marriage can be
distorted. The causes of these distortions are two: the will
of a created being to follow instinctive and arbitrary impulses
only and the pretensions of the State to legislate on the
personal lives of its subjects, their married lives in particular.

The two sources of error often converge when the State,
in its efforts to subdue minds and souls to itself, finds it
profitable to please the people by facilitating the reduction of
marriage to a temporary and purely civil contract.

Pius XI insisted on this when he acknowledged the receipt
of a letter from the king of Italy, Victor Emmanuel, in which
he asked the Pope's advice about a projected law on civil
marriage: "The sacrament is not an accidental quality added
to the contract but is of the very essence of marriage to the
extent that union in marriage is only lawful for Christians
within the sacrament of marriage, without which it is the
merest concubinage. Any civil law which, on the assumption

that the sacrament can be separated from the contract of marriage, claims the power to decide its validity, contradicts the teaching of the Church."

THE GRACE OF THE SACRAMENT

If, then, it is the promises exchanged between the couple that make the sacrament, what greater thing does it bring them? It brings grace, and we shall see how great is the part played by grace in marriage, as in all other acts which are performed in willed obedience to the natural or the divine law.

"Marriage is a sacrament precisely because it is *a sacred sign which brings grace* and which is the image of the mystical union of Christ with the Church. But the form and the image of this union consist precisely in this close bond that joins man and woman to each other and which is none other than marriage itself."

So wrote Leo XIII in *Arcanum*, and Pius XII, in a talk to young couples given on March 5th, 1941, spoke these words in which precision is wedded to authority:

In every sacrament the minister is simply an instrument in God's hand ... he performs a symbolic ceremony, he speaks words which signify the grace which is proper to the sacrament: but it is God alone who bestows this grace, he only uses the man as a minister acting in his name ... and that is why the spiritual power of the sacrament cannot be impaired by the minister. ... But in this great sacrament of marriage, who is the instrument by which God has poured out grace in your souls? Perhaps it was the priest who blessed you and united you in marriage? No. ... [And after reminding them that although the Church requires that the couple be in the presence of a priest he is only there as a witness qualified to represent her, Pius XII continued:] In his presence, it is you who have been appointed by God to be ministers of the sacrament, it is yourselves whom he used to tie the knot of your indissoluble union and to pour forth into your souls the graces which will make you steadfast and faithful in your new duties. [Therefore] does it not seem that, from the first step which you took away from the altar after the priest's blessing, the Lord has willed that you should begin and continue in your part as co-workers and instruments in his work?

[But the consequences of this *consent*, which is an engagement, extend far into future married life. It is a "yes" to all that the future may bring forth. And through all these consequences, in all that is to come, grace will go with husband and wife:] In the sacrament of marriage, the people's acceptance of each other, their exchanged consent made manifest in words is the exterior action which draws down God's grace upon you: in your married life *you will be the instruments of God's craft when he fashions the bodies of your children. You will summon to the flesh of your flesh that spiritual and immortal soul which God creates at your demand*, he, who also bestowed his grace at the demand of the sacrament. And when your first-born sees the light the new Eve will say, with the mother of the human race, *Possedi hominem per Deum*: "I have been enriched by the Lord with a man-child" (Genesis 4. 1). God alone can create souls, God alone can bestow grace, but he will make use of your ministry in order to bring souls out of nothing, as he also used it to give you his grace.

No greater share could possibly be given to creatures in continuing the work of creation. In this act the ends of the marriage union are so fused that the creation of a new life is also and inseparably the true flowering of a being who thus takes his fullest share in the life of the world. But in so doing he finds his own true fulfilment in the accomplishment of the highest act conceivable for a creature—to transcend the limitations of his human state by sending out new creatures into the future, creatures who in their turn will share in God's work, and do so *through grace*.

At this point in our examination of marriage it can easily be seen that if civil legislation attempts to lay down the norms of union in marriage it is trespassing on the rights of the creature itself, of one made by God and worthy of respect because by the actions which are natural to it, it helps to carry out God's plan. But if the creature itself desires to be free of the laws which, as the Church teaches, are engraved in its own nature by God's will, then such a creature betrays itself, refusing its own human creative power, denying its responsibility for the creation of the future. Once again we can see how these totalitarian systems, those legal codes, that claim to speak in the name of the sovereign will of men or of man, are attacking both the freedom and dignity of man and the holiness of those rules of living by which the Church protects and guarantees human dignity.

It is easy to understand what great consequences may spring from this high conception of the dignity of marriage. Modern theologians, therefore, have discussed whether marriage could suitably be called a "permanent sacrament", or renewed at each moment by every act related to married life. A passage from Bellarmine quoted in *Casti Connubii* has been taken to support this interpretation: "The sacrament of marriage may be thought of under two aspects: the first in the moment of its accomplishment, the second in its continuation after its accomplishment. It is truly a sacrament of Christ and the Church."

It is true that as long as the couple live, and live in the unity which is formed by their continued consent, the sacrament continues in its effects and in the grace it brings. But Dom Boissard is right when he says that baptism, confirmation and holy Orders, all sacraments that produce permanent effects, are not thought of in spite of this as being renewed in each act of the baptized or ordained person. Moreover Pius XI cast a doubt on this in a reference to this very passage from Bellarmine: "Christian husbands and wives are strengthened by a special sacrament whose efficacy, although it imprints no character, is none the less permanent." Theology tells us that *character* is imprinted when the sacrament imparts a share in Christ's priesthood, for the purposes of worship. The character imprinted by priesthood, for instance, is indelible, and this is not the case with marriage whose effects disappear when one of the partners dies.

So it seems that recent commentators went too far when they saw in the acts of union that take place in marriage a sort of reiteration of the sacrament. As Dom Boissard insists —rightly in our opinion—acts of bodily union are rather the effects of the sacrament of marriage than the causes of a renewal of grace. We can certainly agree that they may be full of grace if they are performed with love and in accordance with the respect due to creatures and to the laws of life which we shall examine later on. Natural impulses are blessed if they follow the direction of God's will to create. This is a wonderful thing, for it associates even bodily union with the mystery of divine initiation. There is no need to go further, common sense and a reasonable conception of the impulses of nature make it clear that to do so would be to blur the distinction between natural and supernatural.

But it is nonetheless true that from this point of view all the actions of married life from the lowest to the highest, from the most purely spiritual charity to those that are most carnal (and even here charity has a great part to play) are the *occasion* of the ever-present sacrament to work and pour out those graces to which it entitles.[3]

THE HEART OF CHRISTIAN MARRIAGE

To what conditions are we bound to submit in order that the high dignity of marriage, the power of the sacrament which is ever renewed and ever fruitful, may be born out of the sacramental reality of that first day? As we have seen, it is the promise that makes the sacrament. But a promise to do what? To respect the unity, permanence and indissolubility of the marriage bond. Is it enough to think of these as a law, in some sense exterior to ourselves, to which we decide to submit? Obviously not, since we are summoned to make this

---

[3] Boissard, *op. cit.*, p. 89.

submission by the demands of our own nature, of our most essential self, the self which is grafted on to God and will come to its full flowering in him. But the primary law, the very being, of this self is love. There can be no other marriage than a "love-match". What does this really mean?

It would never do, having got so far, to weaken the meaning of the words we use. Yet there are many kinds of "love" match, for love has many faces. As we shall show, it is not true that the Church gives no place to love in Christian marriage. But she knows things that men do not want to know or have forgotten.

The Church knows above all that love is a great, a very great thing—and rare and difficult and dangerous. She knows too how many rash impulses, how many passions, how many selfish desires can wear the mask of love, often without our knowledge. She also knows how easy it is for us to deceive ourselves, in this muddle in which good and evil overlap, in which gift and grab can each pass for the other. And finally she knows that the desires of men are fleeting and that the sun does not always shine on our tomorrows. Therefore she demands, in the name of all that is deepest in us, that we undergo a hard and clear-sighted scrutiny.

It is true and certain that the kernel of sacramental marriage must be a call of love. And neither the Church nor Christian wisdom has ever refused to recognize in the profound attraction of one being for another, to another, one of the greatest realities in the lives of men, one of those moments when a creature rises almost to the level of his supernatural destiny. Therefore the Church desires with all her heart that the sacrament should confirm the consent of two beings who are drawn to each other by love, *if it really is love*.

She has no laws, no narrow legal texts, to define love. The whole story of the Church is the story of love. And as the marriage union is the image of the union of the Lord with his Church so also it is in the language of love, the images of love, in terms of the fact of love—even the most carnal—that all the mystics have sung of their longing for the eternal God.

The Church measures love by the fullness of meaning given to that "yes", by the completeness of that consent which is a promise, quite a different standard from those that are exterior and purely emotional. Marriage is a "society of love, that is, one in which its members are required to love each other", writes Dom Massabki, who among recent defenders of Christian love has given it the highest place.

Does this mean that there need not be passionate, emotional love, that people need not necessarily be "madly in love" at the moment of receiving the sacrament? Yes, it does mean that. But it also means that the two who stand ready must desire to exist for each other, and to serve each other always in the service of what is the most essential part of both—what can truly be called love.

It is in the name of love that the Church and true Christian wisdom advise against marriages of convenience or of interest. But it is in the name of love also that the Church sounds the alarm as a warning against the sort of love in which there is only the will to capture and the will to give, when this mutual taking and giving is not recognized as capable of attaining to real understanding and service of each other.

Dom Massabki has well said that married love "is the love of a whole person for the whole of another person". But it is harder to agree with what follows: "We can define marriage as a complete community of love between two human beings" —or at least we must define our terms.

If it is true that the end of marriage is that ever more and more human souls should press forward into the future and, by their consent to God's plan for them, should completely fulfil the purpose of their being, then this is the standard by which love also must be measured. Modern writers have said that to love someone means to share the other's vision of a common goal. We could also say that it means to want to cause the other to be one with oneself in a common participation in the work of creation which surpasses both. Such are the standards by which Christianity measures human loves, and in so doing it measures them by that in them which is most worthy to be called *love*, to be called *human*.

In *Arcanum* Leo XIII writes about these things in measured terms, in terms of *duty*: "They (the couple) must remember always that they owe each other the greatest affection, unwavering fidelity and devoted and untiring mutual help." And Pius XI in *Casti Connubii* speaks of "married love which becomes part of all the duties of married life, and which holds what may be called the place of highest nobility in Christian marriage". He continues, quoting St Paul: "For faithfulness in marriage requires that a man and woman should be joined together by a special love, a love which is holy and pure; they must not love as adulterers do, but as Christ loves the Church, indeed this is the rule laid down by the Apostle when he says: 'You who are husbands must shew love to your wives, as Christ shewed love to the Church'" (Ephes. 5. 25 and Col. 3. 19).

This is the kind of love that the Church sets before us when she says that love is at the heart of the marriage vow which is raised to the dignity of a sacrament. Far from excluding physical attraction, such love is "charity which is not founded only on carnal inclination which passes quickly, nor on words of affection, but which makes its home in the deepest feelings of the heart and also—for love is proved by its works—shows itself in exterior action" (*Casti Connubii*).

Neither the existence of love (in the sense which people usually give to the word) nor its duration can be ordered. So it sometimes happens that such love is not present in marriage. But what must not be absent is the will to love, a love of good will that desires the other's good and means, with his help, to bring it about.

So we cannot say, simply, and without further defining our terms, that marriage is "a community of love" and that "a community of love from which love itself is absent is inconceivable", for to do so would be to risk making the sacrament of marriage meaningless in those cases (which unhappily do exist) in which physical attraction is in fact absent either temporarily or permanently. But it is true that from the very foundation of the community of marriage it is necessary that the couple should look upon each other with love, that is, should see each other as belonging together, and desire to work together for the common good. We may make use of the phrase "a community laid down" or "established" by love.[4] It seems to express the situation very exactly.

So in spite of everything love is always there, from the very beginning: "God has planted married love in the hearts of man and woman, like an instinct that is inborn", Pius XII recalled in a speech to the International Union of Family Organizations (September 20th, 1949), and he gave an outstanding synthesis of ideas on this subject in one of his addresses to young couples (January 29th, 1941):

A mutual affection born solely of your attraction for each other or of the pleasure you take in the human gifts that you are so glad to discover in each other—such an affection, deep and beautiful as it is, when it is revealed in intimate conversations between those newly married, is still not enough. It is not capable of truly bringing about the union of souls which was the will and desire of God's loving Providence when he brought you together. Supernatural charity alone, the bond of friendship between God and man, is able to forge between you links that nothing can break, neither shocks nor troubles nor the trials that are inevitable in a long life together; only divine grace can lift you above all the little daily worries, above all the differences in tastes and ideas which germinate and grow like weeds among the roots of weak human nature. This charity and this grace—are not these the strength and virtue that you sought in the great sacrament of marriage? Greater even than faith and hope, this is the need of the world, of society, of the family and divine charity.

It is on this basic consciousness of the implications of a love which is aware of our human condition, of its vocation

[4] M. Maistriaux, quoted by Dom Boissard.

and its limitations, that the laws of Christian marriage are built. Human response to love will never be sufficient, never complete, conditions of life are hard, sin is always with us. But the vocation is there nonetheless, and it is on the knowledge of this double need that its laws are based, the laws of human nature itself, redeemed by the Providence of God.

THE CHURCH ALONE CAN LAWFULLY DEFINE THE LAWS OF MARRIAGE

The Church is the only lawful interpreter of the condition of man because she alone has received the words of eternal life. But, in addition, it is she who made the marriage union a sacrament. Hence she has a double title to legislate on its use.

"It is a dogma of the faith," wrote Pius VI in 1788, "that marriage which, before the coming of Christ, was simply an indissoluble contract, became, after the Incarnation, one of the seven sacraments of the law of the Gospel.... It follows that the Church alone, on which is laid the whole responsibility for the sacraments, possesses the right and the power to decide the meaning of this contract which has been raised to the high dignity of a sacrament, and hence to judge whether a marriage is valid or invalid."

And in the same work Pius VI defined the position that the Church had never ceased to hold throughout her history but which she found it necessary to repeat frequently in the course of the nineteenth century, when she was faced with states and legal systems that claimed the right to lay down the laws of marriage according to their own arbitrary will: "In such matters the authority of the Church is so great and of such a nature that no sentence can be passed in matrimonial cases except on condition of following the procedure already laid down by the Church.... So much so that when the civil power passes laws referring to such cases, it can only do so simply as executor and defender of the laws of the Church, following her holy rules at every point and with the clear avowal that it has no wish to include or comprehend in its decisions anything that concerns either the sacramental aspect of marriage or the substance of the contract which is linked to the matter of the sacrament, or its ecclesiastical effects. These are the very words of the Commissioners of Louis XIII in their reply to the clergy of France."

THE CHURCH'S MARRIAGE LAWS NOT RECENT

The first law of marriage is unity to which is linked permanence and indissolubility.[5] Solemnly re-affirming this in *Arcanum*, Leo XIII recalled the words of Christ in the Gospel (Matt. 19. 5–6): "A man therefore will leave his father and mother and will cling to his wife, and the two shall become one flesh. And so they are no longer two but one flesh; *what God, then, has joined, let no man put asunder*." A man marries but one wife. St Matthew is once more called as a witness to these words of Christ (19. 9): "And I tell you that he who puts away his wife, not for any unfaithfulness of hers, and so marries another, commits adultery; and he too commits adultery who marries her who has been put away."

In spite of this people have tried to see in the indissolubility of marriage an unreasonable claim introduced after the time of Christ and his apostles. But St Paul wrote (1 Cor. 7. 10–11): "For those who have married already the precept holds which is the Lord's precept, not mine; the wife is not to leave her husband (if she has left him, she must either remain unmarried or go back to her own husband again)." And in verse 39: "As for a wife, she is yoked to her husband as long as he lives; if her husband is dead she is free to marry anyone she will."

Recalling the "paramount importance" of "the dogma of the unity and indissolubility of the marriage bond according to the law of God" Pius XII explained its "great power to

[5] Canon 1013.2: "The essential properties of marriage are unity and indissolubility, and these have a particular force in Christian marriage because of the sacrament."

bind the family together, to bring progress and prosperity to civil society, a healthy life to the people, a civilization whose light is neither false nor useless".[6]

"Modelled," in St Paul's famous phrase, "on the union of Christ and the Church", how could Christian marriage fail to be "the gift of self—total, exclusive, irrevocable"? (Pius XII, from a speech to young couples, on October 23rd, 1940.)

In this context the two ends of married life have equal force: the birth of a child is only the beginning of procreation, the most difficult part is bringing him up as a being created by God, and it is for this that a permanent home background is so necessary. The time is past when people thought that the work of educating children—both physically and psychologically—could be better done in communal institutions, away from home influences.[7]

But the respect of the partners for each other as persons also demands it; demands that the other should not be simply the means of momentary pleasure or happiness, but that each should remain united to the other in spite of difficulties, worries and sorrows, so that they may each form the other, each through the other and through their children.

Moreover, since the vow is the sacrament from the moment it is pronounced it cannot, "once its content has been fully established by the use of the conjugal rights", be broken by "any power in the world, not even our own, that of the Vicar of Christ" (Pius XII to young couples, April 22nd, 1942). This emphasizes once more the fact that marriage belongs to the natural order and that the Church only confirms its rights in that order.

And yet it is against this permanence and indissolubility of the marriage bond that both emotion and intellect most often rebel on the grounds either that it is impossible to know

---

[6] *Sertum Laetitiae*, letter to the Bishops of the U.S.A. November 1st, 1939.

[7] See the conclusion of this book: the true rights of the child.

today what one will want in five years or twenty, or in the name of respect for the other's liberty.

But it is in the name of human nature itself and "as a natural duty" that the Church never ceases to affirm the need for indissolubility in marriage. Pius XII insists that this is a demand of nature: "What has nature to say on the subject of permanence (of marriage)? Is it possible that grace, *whose action does not alter nature* but rather perfects it, always and in every way, should find any real opposition in nature? No ... the permanence and indissolubility which are required by the will of Christ and the mystical significance of Christian marriage are *also demanded by nature*. Its highest aspirations are satisfied when grace gives to nature the strength to become what it had been taught to desire to be by all that is best in heart and mind" (Speech to young couples, April 29th, 1942).

INDISSOLUBILITY ALSO SERVES BEST THE "FULFILMENT" OF PERSONALITY

Above all there is this longing for eternity, this thirst for permanence which is so deeply rooted in the heart and the unconscious mind of humanity that popular romantic songs in every language are always looking for a way to make "together" rhyme with "for ever". In a valuable passage Jean Guitton shows that "eternity does not make brief excursions into time but accompanies it in slow development. It is lost and emptied of meaning in fleeting moments, those moments in which the individual feels impelled to withdraw from society with its rules and customs; but it is saved and re-discovered in that development over a length of time which leads a person to bind himself by vow, under the yoke of established institutions."

The quick glance, the superficial examination, the inexperienced eye, are impressed by the flash of lightning, by sparkle, by brief or at least limited encounter.

The reason for this is that the passing moment makes it

impossible to reach a real knowledge of the other person. Because it is all over so quickly you do not get *more* of him or of the sensations he arouses in you; there is no time to get to the bottom of what he is so there is still the chance to imagine that one would never get to the bottom of him, that he is even, perhaps, infinite. We do not get more out of a diversity of contacts, but they make it possible not to notice—or to pretend not to notice—that this or that one is a finite creature. They leave us free to imagine the host of possible ones—but each of them will yield us only the surface of his being.

It is easier to seek a little pleasure here, a little love there, than to resist the first demand of the senses which say: change! But it is through victory over these first troubles and traps that love grows deeper. A man who stops digging at the first stone in his way has not cultivated his soil enough for it to bring him a harvest. Like all human work, love does not bear fruit without long labour. He who refuses to labour long will never know the true fruit of love which transforms his very soul.

But he who sets himself to the slow business of building up love will see its grandeur rise above obstacles and sufferings, just as the traveller on a mountain road sees new horizons unfold as each crest is reached, at each turn of the road. But unless he is willing to accept the long upward struggle, the horizon will be hidden from view.

Little by little new spiritual landscapes come into view in each of the partners; territories that were already there, but hidden. To keep on going further, even in the dark, to keep on and on is what reveals the truest depths of love, and there will be flashes of light, before unknown, along the road, that the passing tourist never sees. But we must *will* all this, we must *accept*, we must *consent*, we must *welcome* it. To the understanding heart these words hold more of the meaning of love than ones like *possess* or *conquer*. This is true even at the physical level. Novelty is illuminating simply because it is unknown, but the results of this alchemy of fusion only become apparent in the passing of time, one day perhaps when expectation has died.

So, whatever the appearances, the permanence and indissolubility of marriage are necessary also to the second end, that of mutual fulfilment. Here again Pius XII has put the matter better than we could:

> The indissolubility of marriage is willed by nature for another reason also: it is required *as a guarantee of protection for human dignity*. The common life of marriage is divinely instituted, rooted in human nature; it consecrates the union of two beings made in the image and likeness of God, a union which demands that *they carry on his work of preserving and propagating the human race*. This life in common is very sensitive, even in its most intimate expression: it brings happiness and dignity, it sanctifies the soul, when it rises above the purely sensual by means of a simultaneous and disinterested exchange of a spiritual gift by the conscious and deeply rooted will of both to belong to each other entirely, to remain faithful to each other through all the events and adventures of their lives, in good and in evil times, in health and in sickness, in youth and age, without limit or conditions, until it shall please God to summon them into eternity.
>
> This firm and conscious will enhances the dignity of human life, of marriage, of nature itself, and exacts respect for its laws. The Church joyfully recognizes in this life of married unity both the resplendent dawn of the foundation of the family in the beginning and the noonday blaze of its divine restoration in Christ. *If it is not lived in this way, this common life runs the risk of slipping into the gutter of selfish desire which seeks nothing but its own satisfaction, considering neither personal self-respect nor the honour of the other.* (Address to young couples, April 29th, 1942.)

Those who accuse Catholic thought in these matters of being the child of an inhuman abstraction would do well to read also the words of Pius XII given below. There is poetry in them, as quietly dramatic as in any realistic novel; they evoke hard reality with such simplicity and directness that the tone of an encyclical seems to give way to the communication of emotion aroused by the tragedy of human life: "Look at modern society in those countries where divorce laws are in force, and ask yourselves this question: can the world have a clear conscience when it sees numberless cases in which a woman's dignity has been outraged and injured, trampled underfoot and degraded, wrapped as it were in a shroud of infamy and shame? What secret tears have bathed the threshold of certain doors and rooms! What sobs and pleadings, what prayers and in what desperate tones, have been uttered in meeting places in lanes and footpaths, in deserted passages and corners! No—the dignity of both husband and wife, but above all of the wife, has no better protection than the indissolubility of marriage" (Address to young couples, April 29th, 1942).

This is a fatal blow to those who, enmeshed by biological needs, thought themselves "free". What a factual, down-to-earth "slice of life"! When *one* is not consecrated to *one other* then one of the two becomes simply the means, the instrument of the other, and the most wonderful "moment" becomes a faded rag, a broken toy. For the sake of both the one and the other and for the true work of man which is to build the future, we must give a pledge to the future.

There remains Goethe's "Stand still, fleeting moment, for you are beautiful!" But human life does not stand still, it will be stilled only in death, when time shall have etched its eternal outline.

The intense experience of a moment vanishes with it, leaving only the hurt and the sense of betrayal. Man finds himself when he rises above the passing moment, joining one moment to another as links of the chain which is the life of a man responsible for himself and for his offspring.

In framing her laws, the Church is not unaware that she is concerned with great suffering and that she passes laws on the stuff of deep tragedy. She is ignorant of neither their source nor their grandeur; but she knows also, since she speaks in the name of essential human nature, that the good her laws ensure is greater and more lasting than the suffering they involve.

> Faced with this law of indissolubility [wrote Pius XII], human passions which it has restrained and checked in the free gratification of their disordered instincts, have at all times sought to shake off the yoke, determined to see in it nothing but a cruel tyranny that arbitrarily loads men's consciences with a weight they cannot bear and *enslaves them in a way contrary to the sacred rights of the human person.* It is true that a bond can sometimes be a burden, can enslave as do the chains that bind the prisoner. But it can also be a powerful aid and a sure guarantee, like the rope that binds the mountaineer to his companions on the climb, or the ligaments that bind together the parts of the human body and make it swift and supple in its movements. Such is the nature of the indissoluble bond of marriage. (Address to young couples, April 22nd, 1942.)

So the indissolubility of the marriage bond is not imposed by divine law as a restraint but, on the contrary, as "a manifestation of a mother's watchful love".

The ideas of men are not always as logical as they imagine. Very often the same men, the same climate of opinion, which insisted on the need to order the affairs of marriage first and foremost towards the mutual help and personal fulfilment of the couple, have also demanded the right to "free love".

What Pius XII shows most clearly is the benefit that springs from the indissolubility of the marriage bond, a benefit to the human beings concerned, to the human condition itself: "Among the difficulties, the shocks, the lusts that may lie along the path of life, your two souls, inseparably joined, will be neither alone nor defenceless; the all-powerful grace of God, which is the proper fruit of the sacrament, will be always with you, to uphold your weakness at each step, to sweeten all sacrifices, to comfort and console throughout all trials, even the hardest. If in order to obey the divine law you must reject the earthly joys of which you catch a glimpse in times of temptation, if you must renounce the attempt to make a new life, grace will be there to bring back to you in all their force the promises of our faith, the knowledge that the only true life, the life we must never endanger, is the life of heaven . . ." (Address to young couples, April 22nd, 1942).

THE ACT OF LOVE MUST INVOLVE THE ACCEPTANCE OF ALL ITS CONSEQUENCES

Since it is in and by the procreation of children that the marriage union achieves its ends and its perfect fulfilment so it is here also that the laws laid down by the Church for Christian marriage find their full meaning.

Speaking to midwives Pius XII recalled that when a new life is being formed the whole of the order willed by the Creator is involved:

> In this case it is not a question of purely physical, or biological laws, laws obeyed of necessity by agents deprived of reason, or by blind forces, but of laws whose execution and effects are dependent on the free and willing co-operation of man. *This order, established by the supreme intelligence, is directed to the end willed by its Creator.* It includes both the exterior action of man and the interior assent of his free-will. . . . Nature puts at man's disposal the entire chain of events that leads to the making of a new human life. It is man's part to set free this living force, that of nature to develop it and bring it to its appointed end. When man has done his share and set in motion the wonderful unfolding of life, his duty is one of religious respect for this process, a duty which forbids him to stop the work of nature or prevent its natural development. (October 29th, 1951.)

We can see now what follows from this respect, in and through nature, for the divine will and design which are expressed in it: consent to the marriage union in all its fullness and with all the consequences that follow the central act by which it is expressed, that is the act of love in all its creative dignity, and the joyful acceptance of the child which is to be born.

"Every human being, even the child in his mother's womb, holds his title to life directly from God, and not from his parents or from any human society or authority. Therefore no man, no 'indication'—medical, eugenic, social, economic or moral—can show or give a valid legal right to dispose of an innocent human life *directly and deliberately*, that is to dispose of it with a view to its destruction, whether this is regarded as the end, or as the means to an end which may not in itself be in any way unlawful."

These last lines are very important, for they cover the case where the sacrifice of the unborn child may preserve the mother's health.[8]

When there is a question of killing, even on the orders of public authority, "those who, although innocent, are not, owing to physical or mental defects, useful to the nation", then the Church reminds us that such a thing is "contrary to natural law and to positive divine law, and consequently is forbidden".

"The life of the innocent must not be touched", therefore there can be no attempt on the life of the child still hidden in its mother's womb (*Casti Connubii*).

---

[8] "The Church has never at any time taught that the life of the child was to be preferred to that of the mother.... For the one as for the other there can be only one consideration; all efforts should be made to save the lives of both." Pius XII also said: "Who could judge with any certainty which of these two lives is really the most precious?" (November 26th, 1951).

"If in order to save the life of the mother-to-be, quite apart from her pregnant condition, surgical intervention or other therapeutical application is urgently required, which may, as an accidental consequence, bring about the death of the foetus, such an act could not be called a direct attempt on the innocent life" (Pius XII—Address to the Associations of Large Families, November 26th, 1951).

THE CHURCH FORBIDS CONTRACEPTIVE PRACTICES

The Church is equally opposed to those who would like to forbid marriage to people who run the risk of "giving birth to defective children" (*Casti Connubii*) and to those who wish to enforce sterilization by medical intervention.

Because of this respect for life—but also because of her respect for the natural act and its results—willed as they are by God and ordered by him according to the laws of nature—the Church has always and will always oppose all practices which attempt to prevent the birth of the child, either before or during gestation, in a manner contrary to those laws.

The better to emphasize the unchanging thought of the Church on this subject, Pius XII recalled the condemnation, reported in Genesis, of those who spill innocent blood, for God will avenge it, and he quoted a passage from St Augustine (*de Nuptiis et concupiscentia*, chapter 15) which leaves no room for doubt on the matter:

> The lustful cruelty or cruel luxury of the couple sometimes goes to the length of procuring sterilizing poisons and, if all else fails, somehow or other causing the death in its mother's womb of the child who was conceived there. They want the child to die before it has lived, to kill it before it comes to birth. If a couple have done this, then without doubt they are not worthy to be called husband and wife, and if they have done it from the beginning then they were not joined in marriage but rather in order to give themselves up to fornication: and if they have not both been involved then I dare to say this: either the wife has been a prostitute to her husband or the husband has lived in adultery with his wife.

We cannot quote here all the passages in which the popes have recalled the principles of respect for life, "whether it is a question of life in embryo, or in the course of development, or one which has already come to full term".[9]

[9] Pius XII, address to the Medical Union of St Luke, November 12th, 1944. Pius XII makes it clear in his address to midwives (October 29th, 1951) that "the child, even before birth, is man in the same degree and by the same title as his mother."

Parallel with this respect for life, the Church demands a respect for "a natural power whose structure, and the essential forms of whose use, are ordained by the Creator himself, who also gave it a precise end with corresponding duties which are binding on man every time he makes use of it: the propagation of life and the education of the children."

Three principles govern her position: respect for life; respect for the structure and forms ordained by God for the transmission of life; respect for the ends of marriage which are linked with this structure: the propagation of life and the education of the children, and to this end, respect for the man and woman themselves, considered in their full dignity as complete human beings.

Precise and logical consequences have been drawn from these principles, and much discussion has grown out of them, but now they stand out clearly: abortion can never be authorized if it is a direct attempt on an innocent life. This applies "as much to the life hidden in its mother's womb as to the life already born of her, and as much to direct abortion as to the direct murder of the child, before, during, or after the birth" (Pius XII, address to the Associations of Large Families, November 26th, 1951).

The "fraud committed against the designs of nature which by their very nature express the will of the Creator" is inadmissible.[10] "Even in extreme cases all preventive measures and all attempts on the life or development of the seed are forbidden in conscience and excluded" (Pius XII to the midwives, October 29th, 1951).

REGULATION OF BIRTHS
Within the limits of respect for the marriage union

All this does not mean that the limitation or spacing of births is to be condemned in itself. On the contrary, the teaching of the Church prizes the fact that marriage union consists

[10] Letter of Mgr Montini to the 26th Italian Social Week, September 27th, 1953.

of a series of acts of free and responsible human beings. The Church demands precisely this control by man of his sexual activity. But this control must be acquired and developed within the context of "the apostolate of respect and love for new life", as Pius XII told the midwives. "If there are conditions and circumstances in which, without violating God's law, parents may avoid the blessing of children, such cases of necessity give no authority for perverted ideas, for lowered standards, or for despising the mother who has had the courage and the honour to give life."

There arises here "the difficult problem of whether and in what measure the obligation to be willing to accept motherhood can be reconciled with the increasingly frequent use of the periods of natural sterility (the infertile period in a woman) which seems to be a clear expression of a will which is contrary to this obligation" (Address to midwives, October 29th, 1951). This is the question, so often discussed nowadays, of using the "Ogino method".[11]

The Church's decision is quite clear: "If the application of this theory means no more than that the couple may make use of their conjugal rights even during the days of natural infertility, no comment is required. In doing so they in no way prevent or impede the consummation of *the natural act and its natural further consequences.* ... But if on the other hand it is intended to go so far as to limit the marriage act to those days then the behaviour of the couple needs to be more closely examined."

An intention contrary to the marriage vow

Within this last hypothesis two different cases are distinguished: "If already at the time when the marriage was

[11] The observations of several scientists (of whom Knaus and Ogino were the first) have shown that women are infertile at certain times: from the thirtieth to the twenty-first day before the onset of the monthly period, and the nine days immediately preceding it. See *Laws of Life*, Halliday Sutherland, listed in Select Bibliography at the end of this volume.

decided upon one at least of the two partners intended to restrict conjugal rights to the periods of natural infertility . . . so that on other days the other partner would not have the right to demand the act, this would involve essential defect in matrimonial consent, one which would in itself invalidate the marriage. . . ."

This is a particularly important passage: Pius XII's ruling is based on the mutual rights of the couple which spring from the marriage vow. It is not drawn from simple concern to ensure fruitfulness. On the contrary, it in no way separates the right of both partners to the act of love from this concern for fruitfulness. A previously established intention not to be ready to respond to the other's demand at any time is the evidence he offers of the existence of "an essential defect in matrimonial consent, involving the invalidity of the marriage".

"If the limitation of the act to days of natural infertility" does not involve "the right itself but only the use of that right" (in other words if there has been no previous decision by one or both partners to *suppress* the right "which derives from the marriage contract"), then "the validity of the marriage is not in question", but the couple's behaviour must be judged only on the "moral grounds" of their *temporary* abstention. "The fact that the couple are not violating the nature of the act and are even prepared to accept and bring up a child which may be born in spite of their precautions, is not enough in itself a guarantee of a right intention."

Subordinated to the good of the couple, the family and society, and to respect for nature

In re-affirming the union, the natural bond, which exists in the marriage state between the right to married union (in the marriage act) and the "positive purpose" which belongs to this state, Pius XII has reminded us that this "positive purpose" may only be omitted if "grave reasons, beyond the control of those who are affected by them" render it "inopportune".

The marriage contract which gives the couple the right to satisfy their natural desires, places them in a state of life, the marriage state. Couples who make use of their right in performing the act which is peculiar to their state are obliged by nature and by the Creator to serve as means for the conservation of the human race. This is the special toll which they owe out of a true valuation of their state: the *bonum prolis*—children. The nation, the state, the Church herself, depend in the order established by God, on the fruitfulness of marriage. It follows that to embrace the marriage state, to make constant use of the power which is proper to it and which is only lawful within it, and at the same time always and deliberately to withdraw, without grave reason, from its principal duty, would be a sin against the very meaning of married life. (Pius XII to midwives.)

The wisdom of the Church is very apparent here: she does not teach us to despise this act of love that stirs up such violent desire, such passion, which (after money, perhaps) is the most frequently recurring passion in our lives. She knows that if it occupies a big place in our lives it is because it is linked to life itself; it is its expression and the means to its transmission. She does not ask us to be unfaithful to love. On the contrary she asks us to be *wholly* faithful, and to submit to that mysterious bond by which the future of the human race is linked to respect for the act in which humanity finds its most perfect earthly joy, the only one which sometimes reminds us of heaven.

The use of the infertile period determined by Ogino's research may therefore be considered moral and authorized "even for a considerable length of time, possibly even during the whole of married life" if the motives which lead to its use are "serious, such as those that are frequently included in what are called 'indications'—whether medical, eugenic, economic or social". Such reasons may equally well be "personal, or the result of exterior circumstances": the faith does not in any way forbid—as it is too often said it does—the regulation of births. It simply requires that the methods of regulation should show respect for nature and its laws and that its motives should serve the general and fundamental purposes of marriage. Otherwise "the couple's intention to evade habitually the fruitfulness of their union while at the same time allowing their sensuality the fullest gratification can only spring from a *false attitude to life* and from motives which are alien to the rules of a sane morality" (Pius XII to midwives).

Pius XII boldly defined the principles of Christian behaviour in this matter: "The Church knows how to consider with sympathy and understanding the very real difficulties of married life in our era. That is why . . . we have affirmed the *lawfulness*, and at the same time marked the limits—wide ones in truth—of the regulation of births, which, unlike what is called birth-control, is compatible with the law of God" (Address to the Associations of Large Families, November 26th, 1951).

He explains in the same address that we "may even hope that medical science will succeed in making this permitted method (the Ogino method) reasonably safe". This refers to the difficulty of calculating with precision the infertile periods in women and it leaves no room for doubt of the Church's full acceptance of this principle.[12]

RESPECT FOR LOVE DICTATES THE CHURCH'S ATTITUDE

The principles which the Church re-affirmed on the occasion of the debate over birth control and the Ogino method are those which she has never ceased to apply in all cases where there is a perversion of the marriage act. As commentators on the Catholic idea of marriage are always explaining, the

[12] It seems probable that Pius XII in his address to midwives was also referring to the "Temperature method".

Church's attitude to all this is in no way negative. On the contrary, all she does is to denounce whatever is the negation of the act of love itself, a perversion of its energy, or a refusal of its natural consequences—consequences which bring happiness, well-being, glory, for they belong to life itself. So it is in the name of the dignity of man himself, to whom has been entrusted the mission of creating living beings to be bearers of God's glory, that the Church condemns "all use of marriage, of whatever kind, in the exercise of which the act is deprived by human artifice of its natural power of procreation. . . . No reason, however serious, can make what is intrinsically unnatural conformable to nature and therefore right. Since the marriage act is, by its very nature, intended for the generation of children, those who in their use of it deliberately attempt to deprive it of its power and efficacy are acting against nature" (*Casti Connubii*).

Pius XI recalls that the crime of Onan, which is branded in the book of Genesis, was condemned by the Church as far back as St Augustine. "Even with a lawful wife," he wrote, "the marriage act becomes unlawful and shameful when the conception of a child by it is avoided. That is what Onan, son of Judas, did (Gen. 38. 8–10) and that is why God put him to death" (*De Conjug.* 1, 2, No. 12).

Therefore the Church has "once more laid down that any use whatever of marriage, which, by man's devices, deprives the act of its natural power of procreation, offends the law of God as well as natural law, and that those who do such a thing have committed a serious sin."

This passage is from *Casti Connubii*, and the same encyclical also repeats that priests "must not allow the faithful who are entrusted to their charge to remain in error concerning this important law of God, and, even more vital, they must be armed themselves against false opinions, and must not compromise with them in any way". The Church "admits no departure from the obligation imposed by God's law which forbids actions which are intrinsically evil by their very nature". Whether committed by one or both, onanism is and remains condemned.

But the Church also recognizes that "it is not uncommon for one partner to be more sinned against than sinning". In such a case "when, for a very serious reason (one of the partners) allows a perversion that he or she does not intend, it follows that this partner must be considered innocent, provided that he or she is mindful of the law of charity and does not neglect to dissuade the other and draw him or her away from sin".

Neither is there any "unnatural act" if either temporary natural causes or permanent physical defect make it impossible for a new life to be born of the marriage union.

THE "WRATH OF GOD" DEFENDS MEN FROM THEMSELVES

Since onanism is thus condemned because it is against nature and frustrates the natural end which is child-bearing, all practices and procedures which are intended to frustrate nature and refuse the child are alike condemned by the Church as "abominable practices which cut off life at its very source" (from a letter of Pius XI, *Con singolare*, January 18th, 1939).

Those who refuse to accept nature and its purposes are using their free will against the will of God, they can block its course by their rebellion against God, "and then there is nothing left but the cold, shrewd calculation of pleasure-seeking and inhuman selfishness" aimed at "cutting off a human life which is intended to develop to its full flowering" (Pius XII to young couples, March 5th, 1941).

The power which is man's of handing on life is, says the same address, "a great honour" but one which demands of them "submission to the law of God in their use of it". And in an address to the Cardinals on November 2nd, 1950,

Pius XII also gave an admirable description of how the wrath of God is manifested in the very consequences that flow from the violation of one of his laws: "Such a sin (the sin of onanism) prevents the Almighty hand from calling into existence the innocent souls which would have given life to those bodies and raised those limbs to the dignity of instruments of the spirit and of grace, so that one day they might receive the reward of their virtues and eternal happiness in the glory of the saints." When they reject the law of God the couple are refusing to bring to birth creatures of God who in his presence would have sung the praises of their progenitors. The sinner is punished by the consequences of the sin itself: those children whose birth he has prevented will not be there to plead for him since they will never have taken their place in the procession of humanity, nor carried out the work of their Creator.

Even want is not in itself a valid excuse for restricting births: what is required in this case is "an improvement in living conditions". It will always be a crime to "attack life in any way during the journey that leads from marriage union to cradle: and this includes not only the direct murder of an innocent life but also and equally the attempt to cheat nature in its design which as such expresses the will of the Creator".[13]

All practices—from masturbation to every form of "contraception"—is included in the Church's condemnation. On this point Paul Salleron has written lines which seem to us to have a special importance and finality since they come from the pen of a man who is a scientist both in theory and practice, and since they show how human nature fully confirms the appeal that the Church has uttered in its name.

> Finally, contraception appears to be harmful above all from the point of view of the marriage union. . . . There is a real incompatibility between the total self-giving by which the woman is willing to receive her joy from the man and to let

[13] Letter of Mgr Montini to the 26th Italian Social Week, September 27th, 1953.

him be aware of it and this restriction which is felt as a refusal of something in their intimacy. In the act of love it is essential to give oneself as one really is ... only sincerity in this mutual gift makes it possible to accept without fear the more or less complete loss of self-control which accompanies the marriage act. ... Contraceptive procedures often demand a special mode of behaviour towards his wife on the part of the husband. She becomes a thing, an object, the gift is no longer mutual, it is no longer the fire of love which gives him the right to take his wife to himself: it is a premeditated action and the wife must submit to it. Or if it is she herself who takes the initiative, then she is organizing a defence. If the marriage act gains in "safety" it loses immeasurably in spontaneity; it becomes the object of a sort of bargaining.[14]

When they analyse the act of married love from a completely human point of view, that is, from the point of view of a synthesis of all the human faculties, biologists and doctors reach the same conclusion as the Church: "It does not seem to us that any act can be truly natural unless there is some sense of its purpose, which allows us to take an active, free, and willing part in carrying it out," writes Dr Salleron (quoted above). Human nature is "human" in so far as it is free and reasonable: therefore it freely chooses its ends and its actions by the light of reason. It subordinates its acts to rational choice. Sexual activity itself is made to submit to this idea that we have of our life and its ends. Eroticism is not an adequate end for a human being, either from the point of view of a humanist morality or, still less, of a Christian one, because it is a self-centred and peculiarly brutish end.

By preventing procreation, contraceptive practices attack the very nature of the marriage act. (Many authorities have shown as a result of careful observation that such practices even have a deleterious biological effect on normal sexual activity.) The use of contraceptives violates one of the ends of marriage, and at the same time it spoils the exchange of love between the couple and prevents that mutual fulfilment which

[14] Dr Paul Salleron, *Onanisme et procédés anti-conceptionnels*, p. 47.

grows both from the marriage act and from the children who hold the future in their hands. They are no longer two people wholly united with the whole power of their being, but two wills bent on pleasure, for which purpose each is merely a thing to the other.

CHAPTER III

EROS AND AGAPE

WHERE IS LOVE?

Life begins where love begins. You will be judged by your own life, glorified by your own love. You must make your life yourself and your love will make your life. And there is only one love.

Yet the Church does not say, and has never at any time said, that human love would find satisfaction in its object, nor even that the object would be attained. St Teresa of Avila teaches the opposite, and we have already quoted her crucial words: "There is no remedy for our desire." One of the greatest of modern Christian poets, Paul Claudel, puts these words into the mouth of the woman who is of all his heroines the most complete incarnation of love: "I am the promise which cannot be kept." What is the nature of this paradox, or tragic deceit? This thing, this basic energy of our lives, which summons us and enlightens us, is it nothing but a will-o'-the-wisp, a mirage, a reflection of nothingness?

This question has to be faced: it underlies the whole drama of truly human life. We must have the courage to assert that no human love will come to its full flowering unless it can transcend itself, unless it does not expect its own complete satisfaction from the other, unless it hopes—hopes even to the point of unreason—to be itself all that the other desires. For no human creature can satisfy us, but God only. This does not mean that love can never bring peace, it means that there is no peace in love unless it is the love of God in the other.

And it means admitting at the same time that love can never be completely peaceful because we never completely turn our eyes away from the world itself; because we never completely love the other in God; in fact, because we never finish learning to love God or even to love his creatures. No doubt these words will come as a shock to those who lack faith, and even perhaps to many Christians. And yet the lessons of experience in love as well as the results of all the analyses of love confirm this conclusion. Gabriel Marcel shows it very well: love can never reach fulfilment, something of higher value which is to be served, unless it means communion in the one source which sustains life by giving it a goal which is worthwhile.

But we must set out on this long road—so long that it never ends—in a spirit of love and joy and primarily that means setting out freely, in the freedom of the "yes" that we pronounce at the beginning.

As we have said, the Church teaches that it is not the institution of marriage that creates the marriage union but the marriage union which demands the institution. The law of indissolubility is not imposed on us by the marriage institution, it is our free and loving choice, our free choice in and for love, which itself creates in the sacrament the institution, an institution that binds because its freedom demands to be bound in order to prove its love. Freedom of choice is the first part of the marriage union.

"Although marriage exists by nature as well as by divine institution," wrote Pius XI, "human will also has a part, and a very noble part, to play, for each particular marriage, in that it constitutes the union in marriage of a particular man and woman, has no other origin than the free consent of the couple. This act of free will, by which each of two people give and receive the right which is proper to marriage, is so essential for a true marriage that no human power could possibly substitute anything for it" (*Casti Connubii*).

And the *Code of Canon Law* is no less clear: "It is the consent of the parties, between persons capable in law, which, when lawfully expressed, makes the marriage; nothing can be put in its place by any human power." And again, "Matrimonial consent is an act of will by which each party gives and receives exclusive rights over the body for the accomplishment of those acts which are intended by their nature for the procreation of children."[1]

This "bond to which we are inclined by nature" is not "necessarily dictated by the principles of nature", but springs from man's free choice and is his "sublime responsibility" (Pius XII).

Pius XII insists on this point: "God will wait for you to say 'yes' before he will use his creative power. He, who is master of his own strength, judges with gentleness and rules with great mercy.[2] He will not treat you as inert instruments, lacking reason, like a brush in the painter's hand: He wishes you to make freely the act for which he is waiting in order to accomplish his work of creation and sanctification" (Address to young couples, March 5th, 1941). The "yes" of marriage is also a "yes" to the vast work of human creation, which is entrusted to us by God and begins in him.

CHRISTIAN LOVE GIVES HONOUR TO THE FLESH

This is the marvellous paradox lying at the roots of Christian marriage. In it the demands of nature are answered by man's free consent. From the moment man sets out on an adventure which is his own, which he has freely chosen and of which the Church has made a sacrament because it is the

[1] Code of Canon Law, Canon 1,081, § 1, 2. On these paragraphs rest the cases in which marriage may perhaps be, not dissolved, nor *annulled*, but acknowledged as null, as having never existed. This happens when either the will of the partners has not been *freely* expressed, or they had been united while in ignorance of the real character of the other partner, or because they were not "capable in law" (as in the case of madness at the time of the marriage) or consent was not properly expressed (for instance the nullity of certain secret marriages).

[2] Wisdom 12. 18

way by which man enters into his own life and extends it
into the future of all humanity. Will the man who sets out on
this way be sure of finding satisfaction in it? If he did it
would be death to life, it would shut him in on himself and
his partner. What man receives in marriage is an immense
power to build, the power to be, and to create being through
all that goes to make up life, but first of all through the
union of two bodies.

The Church does not despise the flesh. There have been men
in the Church who did. But, significantly, those in the Church
who did despise the flesh have always been those whose minds
have failed in some way or other to gain a balanced view
of life and of faith. Lacordaire wrote: "Married love, which
is the strongest of all while it lasts, has nevertheless one weakness born of its very fierceness: it cannot be parted from the
senses." And writing of Ozanam he says: "There was one
snare he did not escape. When he felt happy he needed to
share his joy and increase it by that sharing. Dare I say it,
although God *absolved* him by blessing his union, he was too
young for a happiness which is so inimical to great achieve-
ment." But Ozanam was right and Lacordaire was wrong.

No, married love is not a snare, or if it is then all the real
things in life, all the wonderful ways in which life is built
up, by which man becomes truly man, must be called snares,
all the ways in which man, by conforming himself to this
pattern that God has willed for him, carries God's plan into
all the world and helps to make it a reality.

The sacrament of marriage is not an "absolution" given
for the "fault" of the senses. It is God's recognition of all
those acts which will spring from it, including those of the
flesh, right and necessary for the building of life in so far
as they are performed with the intention of carrying out the
divine plan.

But there is no doubt that from the moment when matrimonial consent pledges us to this adventure in which the
senses have their basic part to play, we shall not find ourselves

involved in any very restful way of life, for our free will is from then on at grips with the world.

Nothing is finished or finally answered, everything is beginning. From this springs the hazard of human life, our danger and our dignity; for what we must strive for, in and through marriage, is the perpetual attempt at the conquest of absolute love which can never be achieved. The love which summons us on the first day does not say to us, "this is the end and fulfilment of life", but rather, "this is its birth".

Materialist theories about marriage explain that the sex act is a purely physical one, or that the sexual function is only a function of the body. They equate desire and need. It is true that indiscriminate sexual appetite seems at first to belong to the body only. And yet as soon as a man is even a little bit human he does not demand simply *a* woman, but *this particular* woman. And the woman who fulfils his desire, since she is *this* one, has a right to her own proper existence in the world, she has a right to self respect. This is true the other way round as well. And neither one nor the other can in their union separate their love from its possible consequences, the child who may be born: this consequence is so closely linked with the sexual act that, as we have seen, the act itself is often deformed, degraded, spoiled, deprived of its freedom and fullness, by "contraceptive practices" designed to defeat nature.

So although the sexual act seems to be purely physical at first, it rises above this level as soon as it is regarded as a truly human act, that is, one involving choice and free decisions, and responsibility for the consequences. When the sexual act is purely physiological it is a subhuman act. And can we forget how much more are the first stirrings of desire, the first dreams of love in adolescence, than simply the craving of the flesh? All the poetry of life sings in our ears, people and things shine with a new radiance, under this influence we discover new meanings, possess fresh understanding.

But it is true nonetheless that basically desire is undiscriminating, nor is it only the person who first responded to it who is capable of arousing it in us. And it is also true that the particular person I choose is not all creatures, does not sum up all human qualities—and that therefore all the Don Juans in the world are the unhappy victims of a fruitless quest whose end they have mistaken.

No creature, not even the whole of creation, is absolute. The man who thinks he will find real life and self-realization by repeatedly yielding to the demands of the flesh, never in fact gets below the surface of either himself or the world. He believes he has settled the conflict between flesh and spirit and that in this way the flesh and the spirit will both possess their own order of freedom. He thinks that at the same time he has rid himself of what he calls the "conventions" of society, morality and religion. There have been many famous prophets of this attitude during the last two or three centuries, from Rousseau to Lawrence, from Goethe (at one stage) to Jean Paul Sartre and his circle. But if we look a little more closely we see that this flesh that has been "freed" is not satiated, Don Juan is still unsatisfied, for what he has possessed turns out to be nothing. Simone Weil, who saw deeply into things, wrote that he who "possesses in this way only defiles: to seize power over is to defile, to possess is to defile" (*De la connaissance surnaturelle*, page 14). And the being which is defiled is not the one we desired; instead of opening to us it closes up at our touch. The thing we have defiled escapes and flees us.

THE FLESH EXPRESSES THE WHOLE BEING

But—and Simone Weil understood this too—would the desire of the flesh be so powerful if it were not more than merely fleshly? Neither hunger nor thirst, nor even loneliness, strike so deeply at the heart of our being. The place that desire and love have in our lives allows them to influence all our thoughts, all our actions, our very being. In the quality of a mother's love we can see the nature of her idea of love, from a painter's canvas or a philosopher's works we can discern their thoughts about men, and primarily about love. "If we told people 'What makes physical desire so powerful in you is not a physical thing. It is powerful because you make it the vehicle of that which is most essential in you: the need for union, the need for God'—they wouldn't believe it." So writes Simone Weil, who began her journey so very far from the Christian faith.

On the contrary, the man who separates flesh and spirit finds that he has lost both spirit and flesh. What he gets from the flesh lacks what is essential to it, and the spirit he supposes within his grasp is a word emptied of meaning, a thing without love and far from any human reality. Bridging twenty centuries, Sartre's twin judgements—that man is a useless passion and that hell is other people—parody the words of the Gospel: "What God, then, has joined let no man put asunder." The man who separates the flesh from the spirit becomes, in fact, no more than the "useless passion" that he inflicts on others. The flesh is no longer anything but a prison to him. And between himself and the world, between himself and others, leap the impassable flames of a very real hell, for he has enclosed himself in an eternal solitude. Even in the act of love he reaches no further than himself, or rather, all that he can touch in love is the outer skin of himself. When the flesh is merely the flesh it is a dead end: it is its own prison, a little Gehenna.

Acceptance of the human state is the first step on the road to freedom. As we follow the thousand upward turnings of this ascent, we gradually become able to breathe, in this earthly life, the air which will be the atmosphere of eternity. And the life of the flesh, accepted in its fullness, with all that it includes of awareness of the other, of submission to the demands of the other (even if he is not himself aware of them), and of full consent to the consequences of the physical act, is, for men and women untouched by a higher grace, the

beginning of the lowly and wonderful path that leads to the
life of light.

CHRIST DELIVERED LOVE FROM ITS BONDAGE

These things are so true in human terms that they are to be
seen in the unfolding of history itself. The "eros" of ancient
societies was merely desire self-exalted in wonder at its own
power, never suspecting where its frontiers lay, so little aware
of what it involved that the communities where it reigned
could separate physical love from friendship and from the
marriage union. But as the dignity of man is revealed in the
pages of the Old Testament and far better in the New, so
the unity of flesh and spirit in love is seen as its direct
consequence. The acts of the body are not neutral or indifferent when they express or involve a movement of the whole
being.

There is a paradox full of meaning in the fact that those
schools of thought that attempted to confine sexual life to the
purely physical level have demonstrated the closeness of the
link between sex and the whole human psychology. A childhood impression, an adolescent habit, so psycho-analysis tells
us, can deform the whole sexual life: hence it cannot be purely
physical. His sexual life is one of the essential ways by which
man expresses his will to be, and certainly it is the way which
is most intimately linked to the essence of man, since it
expresses his power to perpetuate himself and at the same time
his submission to unchanging conditions.

We saw at the beginning of this book how much the idea
of "instinct" in man had been abused. But if the influence of
instinct in man is not unalterably laid down, if it leaves room
for freedom, for free will, and hence for grace, the tendency
of the whole idea that we include in the word "instinct"
remains the same—only this instinct makes its own rules. We
must not forget that in man the sex instinct is not confined
to fixed periods of definite length. Jean Guitton, in his *Essai*

sur l'Amour Humain ("Essay on Human Love"), has put this very forcibly in a passage which is very much to the point here: "It all happens as if, in this instinct more than the others, nature had separated desire from need, and that against the best interests of the race. . . . A need whose only reality is that need, is rare"—and at that level man is no more than a beast—"and it is noticeable that it is never coercive. On the contrary desire is so strong that not only does it constantly rise above need but in the place of real need it puts a sort of imaginary apparition of a need which is much more difficult to satisfy since it is nothing but a projection."

MARRIAGE AS THE IMAGE OF CHRIST'S UNION WITH THE CHURCH

The Church tells us of this mysterious, polymorphic, sometimes horrible, sometimes wonderful sexual instinct that when it is directed into marriage as a sacrament we are to see in it the image of the union of Christ and the Church: an astounding idea to some, to others an incomprehensible extravagance, to some few, scandalous. And yet the doctrine has never varied. It is not only at the present time that the relationship of this sacrament to Christ and to the Church has been pointed out. Leo XIII recalls that Jesus Christ himself "willed to make it the image of his union with the Church", for St Paul stated that "the man is the head to which the woman's body is united, just as Christ is the head of the Church" (Ephes. 5. 23 and 32).

And again Leo XIII repeats it in detail: ". . . sacrament because it is a sacred sign which brings grace and which is the image of the mystical union between Christ and the Church" (*Arcanum, divinae sapientiae*, February 10th, 1880): likewise Pius XI (*Ubi Arcano*, December 23rd, 1922): ". . . the holy and sanctifying symbol of the indissoluble bond that unites him to his Church", or again (*Casti Connubii*, December 31st, 1930): "Marriage between Christians reproduces the perfection of union which exists between Christ and the Church." Pius XII never ceased repeating the same theme: "The close and unbreakable bond of marriage is the sign and symbol of the indissoluble union of Christ and the Church" (Address to young couples, August 13th, 1941).

Pius XII also indicates clearly in what way the marriage union is the sign of this: "Marriage is not a natural act only, for Christian souls it is also a great sacrament, a great sign of grace and of a holy thing, that is of the marriage of Christ to his Church, the Church which he made his own and won by his blood, so that these children of men who believed in his name might be reborn to a new life of the spirit" (Address to young couples, April 22nd, 1942).

A passage like this allows us to see what meaning we must give to this very astonishing symbolism: in and through marriage, life is given, is passed on into the future. This life is given by the husband and wife in an act which, although it is a natural one, finds its whole meaning in the fact that, just as Christ established and "won the Church by his blood", so this act is the centre and source of a life of sacrifice consecrated to the task of raising the children who are to be born to a truly human state, that is to the state of children of God.

The most essential of all natural acts—one which, in other circumstances, seems to be the most selfish, an act of conquest, for oneself—becomes in this way the vehicle of God's will and design because in it getting and giving cannot be separated. The husband takes his wife just as Christ "made the Church his own"; but, just as in "taking" the Church God in fact gave his blood to "win" her, so the husband (and the wife in the same way) gives in receiving. The whole meaning of this parallelism of marriage and the Church is to be found at the heart of this mysterious alchemy of giving and getting that is in love.

"The indissoluble and inseparable union (of Christ and the Church) owes its existence to the limitless and eternal love which flows from the heart of Christ. How could married love be, and call itself, the symbol of such a union if it were deliberately limited, subject to conditions, capable of dissolution, if it were nothing but the flame of a temporary love?" (Pius XII to young couples, April 22nd, 1942).

The sacrament of marriage brings grace, we know, but now we also see of what kind it is, and why this grace is perpetual and ever renewed, parallel to that love always new which is the source of grace; it is the grace which makes all that touches the marriage and all that springs from it "truly live with God's life . . . so that man, born of God, shall be no longer a creature merely, but a child of God". The "yes" of marriage is a sacrament and a source of grace because it says "yes" to the permanence of love in a life which is still natural life, born of a natural act, but which is also henceforth and inseparably a supernatural life destined to bring the life of the spirit to the children who will be born of the natural life.

THE WHOLE COMMUNITY

We can surely understand completely now not only why the marriage union is indissoluble but why the lives and education of the children must remain bound to their parents, to the grace of their sacrament, to the graces which will be given them precisely for this education, and because of their enduring love.

Life is already complete, and at the same time it is only just beginning; this love will never end, but neither will its trials. No, none of it ends, not our temptations, not even our falls. But the union of love will continue through all this, and later through the education of the children. A community in grace is born of a community of hope and suffering, because it is a community of love.

The lovers will come to know each other, but in this mutual knowledge they will come to know the world as well; they will know it in their very failures and sufferings. We must *go on*, because it is by going on together that we shall pass through life and pass it on to those we create, weighted with all the treasure it has disclosed and the grace it has cost. And this going on will be a progress in love, in meeting and facing the challenge of a community of the senses serving a community in grace.

There is one point that requires emphasis: it is not the Church which has made a mystery about sexual matters and cut them off from the life of the spirit. Everything we have said so far shows the exact opposite. But the Church has always demanded that we discuss sex in a way which considers its whole meaning. The dignity of man and his whole history is to be seen in the way in which in him, the biological, the physiological (which otherwise might seem akin to purely automatic reaction and quite meaningless) is guided by the spirit and raised by it to the level where freedom is possible. Sexual life is not excluded from this work of building up, on the contrary, it is its very centre. Sex which is merely biological is not characteristic of man; what is proper to man is the free choice which makes sexual life a part of love.

The rules of the Catholic Church for sexual behaviour are not opposed to nature, as we have shown in this little book; they are not even added on to nature, they are the expression of that nature itself, if it consents, if it desires to be truly *human*, that is, free and responsible for its actions.

We saw at the beginning of this book that it was of no use to talk, where man is concerned, about *instinct* without further definition. At this stage we can see, besides, something that even the most materialistic or "Freudian" psychoanalysts are always demonstrating: the sexual "instinct" is only a human instinct when it reaches its own limit, that is when it gives birth to a *normal* love, a love that requires faithfulness to one partner and an indissoluble marriage.

The late Abbé Monchanin before going to India to devote himself to the contemplative life wrote the following, as the fruit of his wide observation of human beings, from the medical point of view as well as others: "There is no irreducible duality in man: there are not separate realms of the spiritual and the material. The life of the body is not of a completely different kind from the life of the spirit. Rather, there is a constant and total mutual penetration of the psychological and physiological lives. The whole life of the soul is a life incarnate, and incarnate in a body possessing sex."[3]

SEX EDUCATION

When, then, the Church requires that sex education shall not be separated from the meaning of sexual life in general, from the meaning and demands of the union in love in the lives of human beings, she is not making a demand which springs from herself, the Church, or from some superimposed morality, or from the requirements of discipline, or simply from a puritanical desire to hide things. There is no puritanism in the Church, nor any liking for an empty secrecy about sexual matters. The Fathers of the Church explained themselves quite clearly right from the beginning. Catholic morality is not of the "fig-leaf" variety. Clement of Alexandria wrote in the second century: "We should not be ashamed to name that which God was not ashamed to create"; and Tertullian put the Christian attitude very well: "Nature should be the subject, not of shame, but of respect." The monk Rufinus (in the fourth century) states that "it is not nature but human imperfection which lays obscurity over these matters", and St Augustine returns to the source of the whole problem: "In its own way and in its proper degree the flesh is good."

What the Church demands in sex education is *respect* for the proper order of human existence: not silence but the teaching of *all* that concerns sexual life. And since this is a matter which is delicate as well as great, it is right that such instruction should *normally* be reserved to the parents: to those who can speak of it with *modesty*, presenting the whole matter

[3] Monchanin, "Sexualité et Morale" in *Problèmes de la Sexualité.*

in its place in the harmonious vision of life which it is their right and their duty to present to their children.

EDUCATION IN GENERAL

It is here that we see particularly the extent of what the Church means when she teaches that procreation is the primary end of marriage. It is not simply a question of physical procreation, we are concerned with the procreation of human children, with the coming into, and *preparation for life in*, the world of beings *designed to be human*.

When, from a purely philosophical point of view, Gabriel Marcel[4] finds the essence of paternity in "the creative wish", he thoroughly confirms the Catholic conception of family life; for, as he shows, the will to have children is the very force of the sex act—to have truly human children, children who will go on into a future in which the parents will no longer be present but in which they wish their work to go on.

All the modern philosophies have developed the idea of the transcendence of life in relation to the world of causes and ends. But it is not surprising if the man and woman who give birth to children have no clear understanding of their intention in so doing. Yet they do want, although perhaps only unconsciously, an expansion, a continuation, of their own being. So the act of procreation is "essentially an acquiescence by which man takes responsibility for, and makes his own the words at the beginning of the book of Genesis: 'And God saw it, and found it good.' "[5]

From that moment onwards man and woman do not want just anything as the continuation of themselves; they want a son who shares their humanity. So his whole education is not only their duty but also their *right*, the right of love. The eternal failure of man to fulfil himself with his own life, man

[4] *Homo Viator.*
[5] Gabriel Marcel, *op. cit.*, p. 163.

perpetually unsatisfied, of whom Don Juan is the sign and symbol, finds in this the solution dictated by love, or rather the second part of the solution, since this procreation and formation of children are love's tomorrow. The procession of humanity goes on its way not only through births but through the *handing on of a message*, which is education. The Church has never ceased to insist that procreation is not a purely biological function,[6] when she demands a "total gift" from the couple[7] expressed in the normal performance of the marriage act. Her intention is to respect their "personal and free cooperation in the act of creation and redemption, and in the fatherhood of God"[8] which can only be achieved through education.

It is not only *natural life* which is expressed in love and which the parents must communicate to their children, but *supernatural life* also, for what they want to bring to birth is a true man, that is, a son and a vessel of God. Of course the parents do not themselves hand on this supernatural life directly to their children. But they want to assure this good to them, and have a duty to do so, by presenting them for baptism and by handing on to them their heritage of faith.

THE DIGNITY OF MARRIAGE AS THE CREATOR OF SOULS

"This marriage union," wrote Pius VIII, "which once had no other end than to give birth to, and assure the perpetual continuance of, a posterity, and which is now raised to the dignity of a sacrament and enriched with heavenly gifts, grace perfecting nature, finds its joy less in the procreation of children than in bringing them up for God and for divine

[6] See especially the address of Pius XII to midwives (October 29th, 1951). This is why the Church does not allow artificial insemination.
[7] *Ibid.*
[8] See Pius XII, address to young couples on November 8th, 1939, October 23rd, 1940, March 5th, 1941.

religion, and strives to increase the number of those who adore the true God."[9]

In the act of love you will give life to children of whom it is said that "the saints are their fellow-citizens and they belong to God's household".[10]

It is for you to see that "a people may be born and brought up for the worship and religion of the true God and of our Lord Jesus Christ".[11]

The mystery of human love can only be understood wholly and in all its glory at that point where it is joined to, and in a sense lost in, the mystery of divine love. God expects us, men and women, to assure that his plan for the world is carried out. And he has entrusted to the act of love the fulfilment of this expectation. He asks us to help him in some way towards the completion of his work, and he asks it out of love; but it is also by love that he asks us to do it. How can we separate these two loves? "What God, then, has joined, let not man put asunder."

[9] Encycl. *Traditi humilitati* (May 1st, 1829).
[10] Ephes. 2. 19.
[11] Roman catechism, quoted by Leo XIII in the Encyclical *Arcanum*.

CONCLUSION

THE TRUE RIGHTS OF THE CHILD

The same refrain has been sung to many different tunes, following many different lyrics: there was the one about the preservation of freedom, which sought to remove family interference in the child's life; there was the song of progress in biology which showed that in the animal kingdom (?) the family "cocoon" was useless; there was the need, since Freud, to avoid regression; and from the same shop came the "Œdipus complex" and the one named after Narcissus. Finally, certainly, and scientifically, the family was the root of all evil, it stood in the way of development and the greatness of man. It must be reduced to its most basic form. A clever writer provided a catch phrase for all this. Gide's "families, I hate you!" became the slogan of an epoch. Also there was some easy laughter over the family as the cell of the social body, and cell was emphasized.

If we needed signs in the skies of moral values, the things that have become known since Gide's death, not only about his own moral habits—though nothing could have been less hidden—but of what these revealed of a terrible "inability *to be*," of complex self-disguising, of shady expedients for reconciling pride and abasement: all this would sound the knell of his "families, I hate you" for it would show up its real meaning—that of a cry of impotence, hatred and death. The concerted evidence of all the inquiries—pediatric, psychiatric, criminal—shows that among those who were ill, maladjusted, introverted, even criminal, the largest proportion were children in some way deprived of proper family life.

The clever Swiss and Scandinavian nurses, the doctors with their sums and ready-reckoners, the book-keepers of souls, even the Calvinist and Freudian ones, they all produced the same conclusions, they all admitted that they had taken the wrong turning: the child without a home, far from being the flower of society and the life's ideal, is marked out as its victim. The very official inquiries of international organizations put their unchangeable seal on the verdict. Even the U.S.S.R. had to return to severe family legislation.

But already a new procession of witnesses appears on the horizon, advancing in close formation. Curtis W. Cate recently quoted the precise figures of the increase of juvenile crime in the United States: twenty-five per cent between 1948 and 1952, and thirteen per cent more in 1953.

The Editor of the *Special Juvenile Delinquency Prospect* (of the Federal Department for health and education), Mr Bertram Beck, says that the problem is not confined to the lower classes and the suburban slums, and he offers an explanation from his wide experience: "Until recently the suburban social institutions—family, the school, church— provided sufficient social pressure to prevent precocious children becoming a disquieting problem. . . .

"Nowadays the wave of juvenile crime has reached all social levels . . . a luminous sign of social decay, and a revelation of the fact that our most solid social institutions are losing their capacity to hand on a sense of true social values from one generation to another."

Quoting this passage, Curtis W. Cate adds: "The crux of the matter lies in the increasing inability of American parents to discipline their children", and he comments: "The worst of it is that this lack of discipline is accompanied by a sort of domestic emptiness. Unlike the French home which is an active centre of conversation, and argument, of animation, of life, the American home has a tendency to become a passive rest centre where a worn-out husband or wife can relax after a day's work . . . a cell whose main window on the outside world is that rectangle of silver screen which unfolds in pictures astoundingly commonplace stories."

So the family is not guilty through being disciplined, loving, even clinging. On the contrary, the trouble starts when it is not sufficiently a family.

THE BOY WHO KILLED TO FIND HIS MOTHER

Other witnesses come forward to corroborate the evidence of specialists and figures, and some of this evidence is the more striking because it shows us living people. An American reporter, Croswell Bowen, specialized very seriously in the study of adolescent delinquents. His work has had the distinction of being used in courses on criminal psychology. He wrote a series of studies of particular cases which provide evidence of dazzling clarity.

Robert Brown spent his life dreaming of the mother he never knew. He stole, he killed, he was incapable of love; wherever he went he was pursued by this obsession about finding his mother. In prison he built up a picture of what his life would be like if he found her again: he would work hard and as soon as work was over he would go home to the little room where she would be waiting for him.

One day, at the seaside, he was accompanied by a young woman with a baby. Near them someone said of him, "That's the father". The "killer" was overwhelmed. Notice in passing the influence, which he recognizes in himself, of the mentality of the gang whose purpose is violence.

The observer adds: "I have frequently noticed this influence, especially in children who are emotionally neglected and exposed to the *sense of insecurity that comes from a broken family*, uncomprehending foster-parents, and long periods in institutions."

Brown told the judge that his purpose in trying to get money by crime was to be able to find his mother; when he distributed the fruits of small thefts to the adolescents who hung round him it was, he said, because "I wanted them to like me".

Fred MacManus, on the other hand, appeared to be a "gratuitous" criminal: he came from an apparently united family. In fact, inquiry revealed a secret flaw, but one which is clear to a child's eyes. He was neglected, ill-treated, only the appearances were kept up. No family, or bad family: the effect is very much the same. One day the lack of balance in the child will suddenly come to light. His mother seemed to prefer his sister, his father only spoke to him when he wanted to beat him. He also tried to make other children love him. His fiancée's family situation was similar to his own, and their conversation always turned on their childhood misfortunes. Here again, the end of it all was crime.

We could quote Croswell Bowen's whole book and add ten or twenty cases from the daily newspapers.

MATERNAL AFFECTION INDISPENSABLE: UNESCO'S INQUIRY

UNESCO recently devoted a group of inquiry projects to the problems of "Education and mental health"; they must be quoted here for they fit in very well with what we have been saying.

First of all, this introductory statement: "The harmonious development of the individual, from the intellectual, emotional and social points of view, is ceaselessly threatened by the collapse of collective values that followed the wars, both fought out in Europe."

When the specialists—doctors, teachers, psychologists— convened by UNESCO came to examine the causes of this collapse they were driven to conclude that these must be sought in the events of early childhood. At this stage, every time the child's actions "produce a satisfying result, every time his excursions into the world outside himself are encouraged by success, he tends to repeat the act and to attribute a positive value to it. Every time that the fulfilment of his essential needs is frustrated by his surroundings he reacts by becoming aggressive or inhibited or both at once."

But we have to be precise about what are the "essential needs" of a child, and it seems that we can easily reach agreement, for the conclusions that the UNESCO experts drew from their observations are compelling. They condemned equally the type of "authoritarian" education which subordinates the child to a "rule" that stifles him, and the so-called "free" education which, either by giving the child the "freedom" to deal with difficulties and problems beyond his age or even by creating such difficulties too early in order to "build up" his character or his will, force him to become aggressive or inhibited.

It is therefore necessary to create an atmosphere of "security"—that is the word the UNESCO experts used—around him. They also stated in so many words that the healthy development of the individual is only possible if "his surroundings provide a satisfying means of expression for his basic impulses, and if he is *supported by the affection* of his mother and family".

Two ideas seem to be especially worth noticing: firstly, that the child needs to be surrounded by a stable and peaceful community, and that the family best fulfils this need; secondly, that the family is not only necessary negatively, to defend the child, but also positively, to help him to become a balanced person: that is what the word "support" means in the UNESCO text.

All the work of UNESCO led them to affirm the overwhelming importance of education in the family, and in particular its importance in the child's "experiences", experiences which may pass unnoticed even by those who are nearest.

> The little girl who appears to be playing quietly on the floor while her mother and a neighbour discuss in low voices the death of the man from the end of the street will, although she

3

may not show it immediately, reflect the anxiety which she sensed from her mother's voice and bearing. If a mother tries too soon to teach the child to eat nicely by showing irritation at his clumsiness, he may end by refusing to attempt anything new which is asked of him because he does not expect to succeed. [From a very early age the child reacts to things which are in no way biological or physiological:] The very regularity of the principal events of his day, his mother's comings and goings, the way she picks him up, talks to him and looks after him, have great psychological importance.

The importance of the relationship between mother and child as the source of the sense of security in the child's development, is emphasized by a large number of recent works. On the purely material level it is not difficult to dispense with the family as the means of providing food, warmth and protection against danger. But recent research has established what psychologists have suspected for some time—that the child's development requires something more than the impersonal satisfaction of his material needs. It seems to be impossible to dispense with the permanent bond of tenderness, confidence and affection between the child and his mother, or the person who replaces her, at least during the first three or four years of his life.

THE MEANING OF ADOLESCENT CRIME

No father, indeed no man or woman in whom remained one spark of human feeling, could have followed without deep pity and horror the case reported in the French newspapers, the tragedy which cost the life of a boy of seventeen, Alan G.

Historians of the future will seek in novels of our period its essential flavour. They will find cases of adolescent crime used as the instrument to fathom human lives and human souls, as in Gide's *Les Faux Monnayeurs*, and Green's *Brighton Rock*. Crime and its records have always served to throw light on history. Famous cases like that of the Queen's necklace, the "Popish plot", and the "Brides in the Bath", reveal the whole temper of an epoch. But these cases concern men, adults usually considered responsible for their actions.

Here, in this real life case as in so many others, and in the books to which they have given rise, the actors in the drama are adolescents, unstable and unsatisfied adolescents. Péguy's famous verdict comes to mind, a comment that stings like a whiplash. "There are no bad sons, there are only bad fathers." Whether this is true of individual cases is always arguable but it is certainly true if we take it as a verdict on our age as a whole. The children of an epoch do not pass judgement on themselves, they provide the evidence by which we may judge the age that bore them.

But first it must be recognized, if we are to form a fair and balanced judgement, that these products of our epoch are not the only ones. Every year thousands of young men and women leave universities, training colleges, schools, and carry into the outside world, into hospitals and factory, schoolyard and shop, to big Catholic action conferences and little back yards, to local Y.C.W. meetings, into office, youth-club, kitchen or barracks, the faith they received in their parish church, the enthralling and demanding task of spreading the light of Christ. But there are the others. Throughout history passion has been a killer: love, politics, power, money—they have had their victims in every age. But our age has produced something new, what Gide called "crime for nothing", a certain icy indifference to the lives or even the existence of other people.

Nowadays some people tend to shrug their shoulders when one talks about the "nihilism" of certain trends in contemporary thought. They are wrong: every day the papers carry the proofs of this sense of emptiness in whole sections of the population, both young people and adults, who feel they are part of a movement without reason and without purpose.

How often do we notice the look in the eyes of the "accomplice" whose photographs we are shown—the boy who provided the weapon, the girl around whom the plot was woven, and others? Those empty eyes, vacant of hate as well as joy, scarcely even a sneer. There is no laughter here, only indifference: "I couldn't care less" written across a whole page of history. I couldn't care less—about life, or death, or love or faith, about the sufferings of others, about the soul or the lack of it. . . . I couldn't care less . . . so killing is easy, and everyone carries a revolver in his pocket. To give life, to take life? What does it mean? What does life mean anyway? Sartre said it was "nausea".

Well-meaning papers have sought the "causes" of such cases as these: children without real families, houses that are not homes, parents who will not act as parents. They are right up to a point, but surely we need to go a step further back in this search for causes. What has happened to these families that they should be so empty, why are these parents so bankrupt in their parenthood?

There is no room for doubt. The evidence fits together too neatly. All this springs from the atmosphere of universal meaninglessness which these children breathe. Love is nothing and has no meaning, respect for the home has no meaning, neither faith nor understanding hold any meaning, they catch no glimpse even of a shared humanity in the eyes that meet theirs, there is nothing there for them that might give a moment's pause to the violent hand.

People have asked what motive could make these boys kill since they seemed to be utterly indifferent, nothing mattered to them. But that *is* the reason: it is possible to kill because nothing matters, nothing exists. That is the point we have reached.

Forty thousand adolescents arrested in 1945, 30,000 in 1947: Why? Because there was nothing left any more. "I couldn't care less." The world we live in is no more lacking in logic than the ages that preceded it. When life is no more than "nausea", when nothing makes sense any more, when two or three ideological trends combine to proclaim that the decision of the State (history, they call it, to give it dignity) decides what is true or false, right or wrong, what is and what is not, then what is left to restrain the hand that holds the weapon?

Look at the pale faces of adolescents who congregate in dirty cafés, who are glimpsed as they scuttle out of the light of a street lamp—expressions that flicker from meaningless hatred to confused vacancy, the wretched little faces of children set in an adult mould before they were ever marked with the experience of being human. They reveal too much, they are the tragic mirror of all our troubles.

We have bred our children on nothing, we have set before their inquiring eyes only an infinite void. Among all the adolescent tragedies of the last ten years—and how enormous the number is—there might be enough cases of children from normal homes to count on the fingers of one hand. Even they had been exposed, perhaps by family insolvency, to influences which were obviously destructive. For the rest, they were the fruit of families that had disappeared, or broken up or been dispersed, of fathers dead or divorced.

These tragic events serve to confirm what scientific research is establishing day by day, and establishing statistically; the need for education in the family. Facts put their seal on professional evidence, but the surprising thing is that men who half a century ago were anxious to base society on the lay community, lacking both law and the love of God, could not see for themselves that by thus doubly insulting human nature they were calling down certain vengeance upon themselves.

RESPECT FOR HUMAN NATURE INVOLVES RESPECT FOR THE FAMILY

It was certainly an insult to human nature, and in particular to the nature of love, to think of it as capable, in the life of society as a whole, of attaching itself in the abstract and individually to all the members of a general brotherhood in which all direct and personal links had been set aside. It meant depriving it of that capacity for free and responsible choice which is the privilege, as also the burden, of the human state. But human nature was also insulted when married love was reduced to a thing of the moment, a means to the immediate satisfaction of the senses, lacking all power to build up the future or any involvement in that future.

However unpleasant these young criminals may be—and unpleasant they certainly are—they, and with them whole sections of people in their twenties and thirties, are in fact victims: victims of the fundamental errors of the previous generation, errors which *have achieved reality in the form of social institutions.*

These things are not said in order to make the guilty appear innocent. They are said so that we may become aware of our social responsibilities and of the consequences they entail. These consequences are in fact twofold. First of all what has been broken must be mended: the family must be restored to reality, to existence even. And everything that can separate a child from his family, or empty it of power or break it up— whether it be a school, an anonymous hospital, or one of those school (or after-school) clubs and organizations which are outside the control of the family—is evil, but evil above all is anything which encourages or facilitates disunity or the breaking up of the family.

The shadows in the picture cover certain sections of the community only—shadows drawn in by certain kinds of books, a certain attitude to life. All these young criminals have sought their ideal of "toughness" in films and crime stories. We shall never know how many souls have been lost in our time through this inhuman obsession, this cult of tough-ness, this back-street gospel according to Nietzsche.

That is the first series of consequences that we have to draw. But there is another. It is becoming clearer and clearer that we cannot speak of "youth" as if it were a whole without marked differences. If our youth includes freaks like the young criminals who get into the news, and their huge band of hangers-on, the great majority are girls and (perhaps even more) boys who look at life with clear eyes and enter upon it with courage.

Nothing could be sillier, or more damaging, than to pass sweeping and quite unjustified sentence on "youth" as such. The remark made above that these "toughs" were back-street disciples of Nietzsche was not merely a phrase. All human beings need a system of thought about the world they live in, a philosophy.

The famous riots that broke out in Stockholm one New Year's Eve are further, and strong, evidence in support of the conclusions we can draw from court cases already mentioned and many similar ones. If five thousand young people "held" Stockholm's main thoroughfare for three hours, overturning cars, breaking window panes, rocking the tombstones in the central cemetery, they were not five thousand criminals, or five thousand freaks. They were the normal fruit of a society that had embraced a vacuum, a religious and intellectual vacuum, all expressed in—one might almost say "incarnate in" —the absence of the family. The Stockholm demonstrators, according to the press, were chiefly the sons of labourers and factory hands, men who earned their living and took home a considerable wage packet. The standard of living in Scandinavia is well known, the horizon is neither misty nor overcast. What is misty and overcast is the meaning of life. For in a country where everything is allowed, everything is "hygienic", there could be no question of "repression".

The great majority of our young people do not know how to give a meaning to life. Cases of juvenile crime should be one more incentive to us to help them to do so. For a century now the teachers of individualism, the followers of Zola, Ibsen, have been proclaiming the rights of the child. Certainly we must proclaim the child's rights, just as we have already proclaimed the true rights of love. It is the child's right to be loved and to enter into life by the only entrance made to the measure of man: that of an enduring love which accepts its own consequences. The true, the great, the only right of the child is to have a real *family* and, as always, divine and human law are united in making it a holy right.

THE FAMILY IS OUR POINT OF CONTACT
WITH THE WORLD

It would be quite obviously unfair to accuse Catholics of paying insufficient attention to the importance of the family unit, its rights, life and reconstruction. It is possible that although we are used to regarding the "defence" of the family as one of the unchanging features of the Catholic programme we are not sufficiently aware of the family as something that makes a link between our faith and the world, that roots in it the world, bearing witness before the world of what life means to the Christian. If it is attacked, misrepresented or misunderstood the whole Catholic concept of existence and of the world is immediately degraded, or even destroyed with it.

But if proof is needed, contemporary events are enough to open our eyes and bring us to our senses. However little attention we pay to it the fact remains that every influence which, consciously or not, is aimed at undermining the Christian faith in the modern world first attacks the sense of family. The atheist philosophers came to grips with it and still do: some, like Freud, and all the devotees of physiology, tried to reduce the family to an essence of purely biological relationships of material value only; others, of whom Sartre is the most recent example, tried to make out that even these biological relationships had no more than an excretory function.

Not a few political and social systems have followed the same line. Individualism recognized only man "born a foundling and dead a bachelor". Totalitarianism reduced parenthood to a purely procreative function and pursued like the plague anything that tended to produce a sense of continuity or authority in the family, or any function or meaning other than (once again) purely material ones. When we look (as we have to and must do) for some criterion by which to judge between totalitarian régimes and those that show respect for the person, between those ideologies that can and cannot be reconciled with the Faith, there was and is one which is safe and clear: what do they think of the family?

All over the world a great movement is developing, a regained sense of the family. It is not only a defensive movement but one springing from a new and deeper consciousness, in some cases even a new discovery.

Instead of the myth of love outside marriage, the watered down romanticism of nineteenth-century novelists with their conventional unconventionality, their earnest glorification of a promiscuity from which even the shadow of gaiety had departed, we have uncovered the reality of love: difficult, laborious—but creative. It is happening under our eyes—the tide water of truth sweeping in to restore life to the parched shore whose creatures seemed about to die for lack of their natural element. The family which is a family in name only, shrivelled, meaningless, lacking strength or power, apparently bound to succumb to the forces that attack it, is suddenly transformed. This is a new creation: the family that belongs to eternity, young in hope, armoured in faith, confident of glory, determined to be fully itself and nothing but itself.

THE FAMILY, SOURCE OF JOY

We have had the cynical jokes of Coward's plays, of the "emancipated" novelists of the twenties, smugly laughing at the tyranny of married life, acclaiming the freedom of "bohemian" housekeeping with its shifting partnerships, its "sensible" divorces. The new generation of writers no longer finds marriage merely a bad joke, experience has made them seek the material of drama, even of tragedy, not in the quest for fulfilment by escaping from the suffocating domestic prison, but in the real tragedy of couples whose heritage bars them from finding the happiness they rightly seek in marriage. Marriage is something worth working at, therefore its failure is tragic, the failure to find in it their true vocation, their real unity.

Here and now we are in the thick of the greatest battle of all history, a battle whose outcome is of eternal consequence. But the scene is still lit only by the first dawn sunshine.

Our first defence, our surest weapon, in this battle which is the battle of love, is the truth of our way of thinking, and of our motives. The fresh and glorious flowering of married life and of child-bearing will only be truly fruitful if it springs from the right root; a healthy, rightly instructed understanding of family life. And because it is so rooted it grows sturdily to full and upright beauty. From time to time something happens that brings fresh assurance of this completeness and right purpose. It is no small triumph when a master in the fields both of science and the humanities, Professor E. de Greeff, writes as follows in a recently published book, lines which go right to the heart of the struggle: "Is it impossible to make people understand nowadays that if they must have children it is not because the Government needs them, but simply because it is their normal destiny as men to have them, that their souls will reach fulfilment and maturity under the sign of the child and that if they are magnanimous enough to extend towards other men the protection and love that they will discover in themselves for their children, they will have created a better future for the world at the same time that they found the salvation of their own being?"

MAN'S FULFILMENT

This is the right level at which to consider family responsibility. Whatever the intention, the fact remains that because the heart of this care and responsibility was attacked, because, that is, the heart of man himself was attacked, struck in what binds him to his destiny and to the world, which gives meaning to his life and links him to the rest of creation and of its creator, the idea of the family itself was eaten away or opposed. But when its whole and essential meaning is made clear then it regains its strength, it is not merely defended but nourished and newly created from moment to moment. Here again speaks Professor de Greeff:

> True subordination, that which is formed in love and bears fruit in parenthood, involves subordination to the race through subordination to the child. Man is biologically subordinate to the race, that is his destiny. Parenthood is the direct, obvious and well-marked road by which he reaches his biological destiny in pursuing his moral destiny. [The family and parenthood can never for an instant be considered as a means to serve something else, but only our own destiny, that is, our fulfilment in God by his love.] The fact, the intimate, secret, infinitely delicate yet infinitely great fact, that a father and mother will subordinate their whole life without hesitation to the needs of the new-born child, and find in this the only possible attitude, the basis of their way of life from day to day, seems quite unknown to some defenders of the family. To them parental love is an almost animal thing, a thing of so little value that they claim the right, once the children have been reared, to dispose of them without holding themselves in any way accountable to their family.

On the contrary, the family is the place in which the children are made ready to go out into life and, inseparably linked to this, the parents find the completion of their lives—and we have already seen the wholly spiritual meaning which is here given to this idea of completion. De Greeff has had the courage to say, and say rightly, that to live without going to all lengths in one's subordination to love is to be self-condemned to a life which lacks the vision of the world that is proper to the complete man, and he concludes that any science of human nature which is in conformity with normal psychology must respect the psychology of the *couple*, "without which a completed personality is scarcely possible".

These are the statements of a man of science in the middle of the twentieth century. The family is man himself, the essential means for the working out of his destiny, the point at which he must give or refuse himself, at which he begins his journey to God, at which God acknowledges him, measures his love, draws him to himself or abandons him. It is the way of man in God and of God in man. This is the thing we have to defend, but first of all we have to understand and live it, for if we do not understand and live it no defence is possible, none that does not merit the Marxist accusation of "mystification". "When we speak of the family we are speaking of ourselves and of our own being," writes Jean Lacroix. It is the point at which everything is decided for each of us individually, but here also our fate as a race is decided, and the fate of the modern world.

Here, as in every other place, the Christian faith which was able to transform Eros into Agape because it alone was capable of giving to love its full meaning and an institution whose structure was able to carry the fullness of that meaning—here, as in every place, the Christian faith through its laws brings man to his full manhood.

The reason is clear enough. The bankruptcy of the family is the great evil of mankind. We must draw the correct conclusions from this fact: in the life of the community the family must be served before all. First comes family housing. Whatever serves this purpose, whatever conserves it and also whatever brings it opportunity must be the legislator's first concern. It should be possible for the family to choose the school and so preserve the integrity of the children's education. And the atmosphere of the larger social unit should not encourage division in the family. That is the basic problem of the twentieth century, and we ought to have the courage to show it up. There is one fact which has an urgent reality, which matters every day, a scientific fact, and that is that if the family is impaired man himself is impaired. And there is only one human law that has ever served the family—the Christian idea of marriage.

SELECT BIBLIOGRAPHY

GUITTON, Jean: *Essay on Human Love*, London, Rockliff, 1951.

JOYCE, George H., S.J.: *Christian Marriage*, London and New York, Sheed and Ward, 1954.

LEEMING, Bernard, S.J.: *Principles of Sacramental Theology*, London, Longmans, and Westminster, Md, Newman Press, 1956.

MCNAB, Vincent, O.P.: *Casti connubii, Encyclical Letter of Pius XI on Christian Marriage*, with commentary, London and New York, Sheed and Ward, 1933.

MURPHY, J. P. and LAUX, J. D.: *The Rhythm Way to Family Happiness*, 2nd ed., New York, Hawthorn Books, 1955.

MESSENGER, Ernest C.: *Two in One Flesh*, 3 volumes, London, Sands, 1948 and Westminster, Md, Newman Press, 1955 (3 volumes in one).

SUTHERLAND, Halliday: *Laws of Life*, London and New York, Sheed and Ward, 1935.

THIBON, Gustave: *What God has joined Together*, London, Hollis and Carter, and Chicago, Regnery, 1952.

THOMAS, John L.: *Marriage and Rhythm*, Westminster, Maryland, Newman Press, 1957.

WAYNE, T. G.: *Morals and Marriage: the Catholic Background to Sex*, London and New York, Longmans, 1936.

The Twentieth Century Encyclopedia of Catholicism

The number of each volume indicates its place in the over-all series and not the order of publication.

PART ONE: KNOWLEDGE AND FAITH

1. What Does Man Know?
2. Is Theology a Science?
3. The Meaning of Tradition
4. The Foundations of Faith
5. Does the Faith Change?
6. What is Faith?
7. God's Word to Man
8. Myth or Mystery?
9. What is a Miracle?
10. Is There a Christian Philosophy?
11. Early Christian Philosophy
12. Medieval Christian Philosophy
13. Modern Thought and Christian Philosophy
14. Does Christianity Oppose Science?
15. The God of Reason

PART TWO: THE BASIC TRUTHS

16. The Worship of God
17. What is the Trinity?
18. The Holy Spirit
19. In the Hands of the Creator
20. The Problem of Evil
21. Who is the Devil?
22. The Slavery of Freedom
23. The Theology of Grace
24. The Word Made Flesh
25. What is Redemption?
26. The Communion of Saints
27. The Basic Virtues
28. The Resurrection of the Body

PART THREE: THE NATURE OF MAN

29. The Origins of Man
30. Evolution
31. What is Man?
32. What is Life?
33. What is Psychology?
34. Man in His Environment
35. What is Metaphysics?
36. Psychical Phenomena

PART FOUR: THE MEANS OF REDEMPTION

37. Prayer
38. The Nature of Mysticism
39. Spiritual Writers of the Early Church
40. Christian Spirituality of the Middle Ages
41. Post-Reformation Spirituality
42. Spirituality in Modern Times
43. Pilgrimages and Their Meaning
44. Mary The Mother of God
45. The Marian Cult
46. What is a Saint?
47. What is an Angel?

PART FIVE: THE LIFE OF FAITH

48. What is the Church?
49. What is a Sacrament?
50. Christian Initiation
51. The Forgiveness of Sins
52. The Bread of Life
53. What is a Priest?
54. Christian Marriage
55. The Death of a Christian
56. Christian Morality
57. Christian Social Teaching
58. World Morality
59. Christianity and Money

PART SIX: THE WORD OF GOD

60. What is the Bible?
61. The Promised Land
62. Biblical Archeology
63. Biblical Criticism
64. God's People in the Bible
65. The Religion of Israel
66. Messianic Prophecies
67. How Do We Know Jesus?
68. The Life of Our Lord
69. What is the Good News?
70. St. Paul and His Message
71. What the Old Testament Does Not Tell Us
72. What the Gospels Do Not Tell Us
73. The Jewish Faith

TWENTIETH CENTURY ENCYCLOPEDIA OF CATHOLICISM

PART SEVEN: THE HISTORY OF THE CHURCH

74. The Revolution of the Cross
75. The Early Middle Ages
76. The Later Middle Ages
77. The Reformation and the Counter-Reformation
78. The Church in the Eighteenth Century
79. The Nineteenth Century and After

PART EIGHT: THE ORGANIZATION OF THE CHURCH

80. What Is Canon Law?
81. The Papacy
82. The Government of the Church
83. Successors of the Apostles
84. The Christian Priesthood
85. Religious Orders of Men
86. Religious Orders of Women
87. The Laity's Place in the Church
00. The Catholic Spirit

PART NINE: THE CHURCH AND THE MODERN WORLD

89. Church and State
90. The Church in World Economy
91. Contemporary Atheism
92. Science and Religion
93. Christianity and Psychiatry
94. Christianity and the Machine Age
95. Christianity and the Space Age
96. Christianity and Communism
97. Christianity and Colonialism
98. The Church Works Through Her Saints
99. History of the Missions
100. Missions in Modern Times
101. Religious Sociology
102. The Mission of the Church in the World
103. The Church and Sex
104. The Workers of the Church
105. Charity in Action
106. Christianity and Education
107. Why We Believe

PART TEN: THE WORSHIP OF THE CHURCH

108. The Spirit of Worship
109. The Books of Worship
110. History of the Mass
111. The Liturgical Revival
112. Western Liturgies
113. Eastern Liturgies
114. Vestments and Church Furniture

PART ELEVEN: CATHOLICISM AND LITERATURE

115. The Writer in God's Service
116. Sacred Languages
117. Early Christian Literature
118. Christian Literature of the Middle Ages
119. Christian Humanism
120. Christianity and Modern Thought
121. Sin and Grace in Modern Literature

PART TWELVE: CATHOLICISM AND ART

122. The Christian Meaning of Art
123. The Origins of Christian Art
124. Abbeys and Cathedrals
125. Church Architecture
126. Christian Painting
127. Christian Sculpture
128. Stained Glass
129. Modern Sacred Art
130. Christian Theatre
131. Christian Music
132. The Motion Picture and Faith
133. Radio, Television and Christianity
134. The Catholic Press

PART THIRTEEN: OUTSIDE THE CHURCH

135. Greek and Russian Orthodoxy
136. Heresies and Heretics
137. Protestantism
138. The Ecumenical Movement
139. Modern Sects

PART FOURTEEN: NON-CHRISTIAN BELIEFS

140. Primitive Religions
141. Religions of the Ancient East
142. Greco-Roman Religion
143. The Religion of Mohammed
144. Hinduism
145. Buddhism
146. Mystery Cults
147. Superstition
148. The Rationalists

PART FIFTEEN: GENERAL AND SUPPLEMENTARY VOLUMES

149. Why I am a Christian
150. Index

All titles are subject to change.